The World
of
CHOCOLATE

Risotto of wild Scottish mushrooms with a savoury Parmesan cheese basket

Ingredients

- 150g cleaned wild mushrooms – eg girolles (chanterelles), trompette, ceps – broken into even-size pieces
- 200g of risotto rice
- 1 glass dry white wine
- 2 finely-chopped shallots
- 1/2 litre of mushroom stock or made-up vegetable stock cube
- 50g butter to start, 60g to finish
- 60g freshly-grated Parmesan cheese to finish the risotto
- Optional truffle oil, or virgin olive oil
- 150g Parmesan for cheese basket

Method

Place 50g butter, shallots in a saucepan and cook lightly for one minute.

Add rice and warm it, stirring all the time. Add the mushrooms, wine and stock gradually, stirring at all times, until such time as the rice is cooked, and so that it is of a creamy consistency and to your own taste.

Season, add rest of butter and Parmesan cheese and stir through.

Add small drop of optional truffle oil, or virgin oil and stir for a while to make it creamy (it may need a little more stock).

Cheese basket

Take a small non-stick pan and sprinkle Parmesan into a circle.

Place under a hot grill until it is lightly coloured and forms a small disc.

Flip it over a cup to form it into a basket shape.

Brioche and cranberry chocolate bread and butter pudding with praline ice cream

Makes six demi-tasse coffee mugs

Ingredients

For the custard
- 1 egg
- 100ml milk
- 150ml cream
- 125g sugar
- 50g cocoa powder
- 50ml coffee liqueur
- 32 fresh cranberries
- Brioche for four, cubed

Method
Whisk all ingredients together, coat coffee mugs with butter and sugar (to avoid sticking). Cut enough brioche to fill the coffee mugs and push five or six fresh cranberries, through the brioche, into each.

Then fill each mug with the custard and allow to sit for one hour. Bake at gas mark 6 (200C, 400F) for 20 minutes.

For the praline
- 125g roasted, unskinned almonds
- 125g roast skinned hazelnuts
- 230g caster sugar

Method
Place sugar in a heavy based pan, stir slowly with a wooden spoon until sugar dissolves (pay careful attention to the sugar or else it may burn).

Slowly agitate the sugar until it turns golden brown.

Remove from heat, stir in the almonds and hazelnuts.

Pour on to a greased baking sheet.

When it has thoroughly cooled, it can be broken up and stored in an airtight tin until required.

Praline ice cream
- 570ml milk
- 4 to 6 egg yolks
- 140g caster sugar
- Vanilla pod or vanilla essence
- 280ml cream

Bring milk and vanilla pod to the boil.

Separate the egg yolks and beat them with the sugar until it coats the back of a spoon.

Take 1/3 of the milk from the pan and beat in egg yolks, stir well, then return to pan, stirring all the time.

Stir until the mixture starts to thicken (without actually boiling). When it coats the back of the spoon, remove from heat.

The mixture should now be

strained through a fine sieve; remove vanilla pod. The mixture should now be cooled rapidly by placing it in a bowl of iced water.

Put in ice cream maker to revolve and almost freeze.

Add the cream to the mixture and continue to mix until smooth.

Add praline to mixture.

3: Breast of duck with fondant root vegetables, creamed cabbage and red wine sauce

Autumn is the time of year to search out wild mushrooms (whether from the deli or the woods) and you'll need some for Caledonian Hotel executive head chef **Alan Matthews**' starter of risotto of wild mushrooms served in a cheese basket, followed by breast of duck with a fondant of root veg. And for sweet tooths there's brioche and cranberry bread and butter pudding with praline ice cream.

Method

Score fat on the six duck breasts as much as possible.

Season with salt and pepper, and a pinch of five spice.

Cook in a heavy-based pan, fry on both sides for a couple of minutes until skin side is golden brown and crispy.

Cook for a further three minutes on each side in the oven at gas mark 6/200C.

Take duck from oven to rest for at least ten minutes.

To cook root vegetables

Peel and cut veg into even-sized chunks.

Place in a heavy-based pan, just cover with water, season well with salt, pepper and a sprig of thyme.

Add butter and bring to boil, cook until water evaporates.

Allow butter to turn golden brown and vegetables to colour lightly. If they are still hard, top up with a small amount of water and continue to cook.

Creamed cabbage

Boil the cabbage until cooked, squeeze dry with rubber gloves and while still hot chop finely in a blender.

Place cabbage in pan, add cream and butter and season to taste. It needs to resemble the consistency of mashed potato.

For the red wine sauce

Place the shallots, red wine, port, peppercorns and clove into pan and reduce by two thirds.

Add veal stock, reduce by half, season to taste, then whisk through butter.

Ingredients

● Six duck breasts, salt, pepper and five spice

For the root vegetables

● 2 large carrots, 1 swede, 1 head of celeriac, 2 large parsnips, knob of butter, salt, pepper and a sprig of thyme

For the creamed cabbage

● 1/3 medium size spring or savoy cabbage (stalk removed), 100ml cream and 30g butter, salt and pepper

For the red wine wauce

● 3 glasses of dry red wine, 1 large glass of red port,
2 shallots (finely sliced), 2 crushed black peppercorns, 1 clove
300ml veal stock (or equivalent in made-up meat stock cube)
30g butter, seasoning

The World
of
CHOCOLATE

*A fascinating guide to
the food of the gods*

Christine McFadden

HERMES
HOUSE

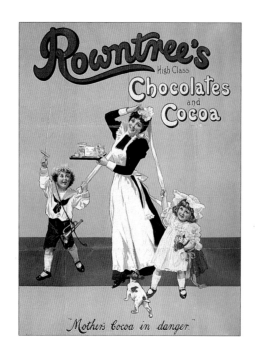

This edition published in 1999 by Hermes House

© Anness Publishing Limited 1998, 1999

Hermes House is an imprint of
Anness Publishing Limited
Hermes House
88–89 Blackfriars Road
London SE1 8HA

ISBN 1 84038 291 0

A CIP catalogue record for this book is available from the British Library.

Publisher: Joanna Lorenz
Project Editor: Joanne Rippin
Assistant Editor: Emma Gray
Designer: Nigel Partridge
Special Photography: Don Last
Picture Researcher: Vanessa Miles
Editorial Reader: Felicity Forster
Production Controller: Ann Childers

Previously published as part of a larger compendium, *The World Encyclopedia of Chocolate*

Printed and bound in Singapore

1 3 5 7 9 10 8 6 4 2

Contents

THE HISTORY OF CHOCOLATE

DRINK OF THE GODS

The origins of the solid, sensuous and, to some, addictive substance we know as chocolate are rooted in New World prehistory in the mysterious realm of the Olmec and the Maya. It was these ancient Mesoamerican civilizations living in the heart of equatorial Central America who were responsible for cultivating the tree from which chocolate is derived.

THE OLMEC

Three thousand years ago the Olmec people, one of the earliest Mesoamerican civilizations, occupied an area of tropical forests south of Veracruz on the Gulf of Mexico. Modern linguists have managed to reconstruct the ancient Olmec vocabulary and have found that it includes the word "cacao". Given the cacao tree's requirement for hot, humid and shady conditions, such as the land of the Olmecs, many historians are certain that the first civilization to cultivate the tree was the Olmec, and not the Aztecs, as is commonly believed.

THE MAYA

Around the fourth century AD, several centuries after the demise of the Olmec, the Maya had established themselves in a large region just south of present-day Mexico, stretching from the Yucatán peninsula in Central America across to the Chiapas and the Pacific coast of Guatemala. The humid climate there was perfect for the cacao tree, and it flourished happily in the shade of the tropical forest.

The Maya called the tree *cacahuaquchtl* – "tree" – as far as they were concerned, there was no other tree worth naming. They believed that the tree belonged to the gods and that the pods growing from its trunk were an offering from the gods to man.

LEFT: The Maya wrote their books on folding screens of bark paper. These two pages show a black-faced merchant god with cacao growers.

BELOW: Fifteenth-century Aztec stone figure holding a cacao pod.

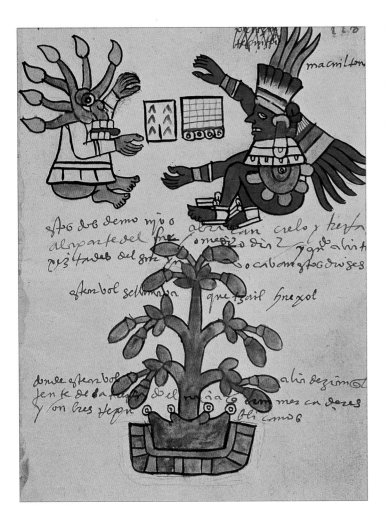

ABOVE: This pre-Columbian codex shows Theobroma cacao, *with its pods, growing in a soil-filled sink-hole.*

The period around AD 300, known as the Classic Mayan civilization, was a time of great artistic, intellectual and spiritual development. The Maya built magnificent stone palaces and temples, carving into the sacred walls images of cacao pods – for them the symbol of life and fertility.

Known as "the people of the book", the Maya also devised a system of hieroglyphics, which were written down on fragile sheets of bark paper. Today only four of the Maya's books

—————————————————————————————

— *THEOBROMA CACAO* —

The eighteenth-century Swedish botanist Linnaeus, who invented the binomial system of classification for all living things, later named the tree *Theobroma cacao,* meaning "drink of the gods", from the Greek *theos* (god) and *broma* (beverage). He felt it deserved a name that reflected the Mayan belief that the tree belonged to the gods, rather than the New World name of cacao or chocolate tree.

—————————————————————————————

survive, and these are all from the post-Classic period. The books are full of drawings of gods who are depicted performing various religious rituals in which cacao pods frequently appear, and the text often refers to cacao as the god's food.

The Maya were the originators of a bitter brew made from cacao beans. This was a luxury drink enjoyed by kings and noblemen, and also used to solemnize sacred rituals. In their books the Maya describe several ways of making and flavouring the brew. It could be anything from porridge thickened with ground maize meal, to a thinner concoction for drinking. An early picture shows the dark brown liquid being poured from one vessel to another to produce an all-important froth. Various spices were used as flavourings, the favourite being hot chilli.

More evidence of Maya use of cacao survives on the many painted vessels that have been unearthed from their burial grounds. A tomb excavated in Guatemala in 1984 contained several vessels obviously used for chocolate drinking. One exotic and beautiful specimen bears the Mayan symbol for chocolate on its lid and was found still to contain residues of the drink.

THE TOLTECS AND AZTECS

After the mysterious fall of the Mayan empire around AD 900, the gifted and supremely civilized Toltecs, later followed by the Aztecs from Mexico, settled in former Mayan territory. Quetzalcoatl, the Toltec king, was also believed to be the god of air, whose mission was to bring the seeds of the cacao tree from Eden to man and to teach mortals how to cultivate various crops.

Because of political uprisings, Quetzalcoatl and his followers left the capital and fled south to the Yucatan. During a period of ill health he was persuaded to drink a mysterious cure, which, in fact, drove him insane. Convinced he must leave his kingdom, Quetzalcoatl sailed away on a small raft, promising to return in a preordained year to reclaim his kingdom. The legend of his exile became part of Aztec mythology, and astrologers predicted that in 1519 a white-faced king would return to release his people. This belief was to influence the whole future of the New World.

RIGHT: Aztecs greeting the white-skinned explorers landing on the coast of Tabasco. The Aztecs believed they were gods returning to recover their kingdom.

THE SPANISH ADVENTURERS

Although the Spanish explorer Hernán Cortés is generally considered to be the first European to recognize the potential of Aztec chocolate, the initial discovery must be attributed to Christopher Columbus. In 1502, on his fourth and final voyage to the Caribbean, Columbus reached the island of Guanaja off the Honduran coast. The story goes that he was greeted by Aztecs who offered him a sackful of what looked like large almonds in exchange for some of his own merchandise. Noticing his puzzlement, the Aztecs explained that a very special drink, *tchocolatl* (or *xocolatl),* could be made with these beans. Their chief demonstrated by having his servants prepare some on the spot. Columbus and his crew found the resulting dark and bitter concoction repellent but nevertheless took some cacao beans back to Spain for curiosity value, little realizing their future economic worth.

ABOVE: Hernán Cortés, the Conquistador.

CACAO AS CURRENCY

When Hernán Cortés arrived in the New World seventeen years later, Montezuma II, the then Aztec Emperor, believed Cortés to be a reincarnation of Quetzalcoatl, the exiled Toltec god-king whose return had been predicted to take place in the same year. The confusion made it easy for Cortés to gain access to Tenochtitlán, the Aztec capital, where Montezuma received him and his men with a royal welcome. The emperor offered them numerous gifts, including a cacao plantation, and an extravagant banquet was prepared in their honour.

Despite the overwhelming welcome, Montezuma eventually realized that he had made a mistake and had wrongly identified the Spaniard. Immediately recognizing the insecurity of his position, Cortés enlisted the help of sympathetic natives and managed to take Montezuma prisoner. Within the space of two or three years he brought about the downfall of the Aztec kingdom. Unlike Columbus, Cortés quickly realized the enormous economic value of the cacao bean, both as food and a form of currency. A contemporary of Cortés reported that a slave could be bought for one hundred cacao beans, the services of a prostitute for ten, and a rabbit for four. The Jesuit, Pedro Martyre de Angleria, called the beans "pecuniary almonds" and described them as "blessed money, which exempts its

ABOVE: A painting showing Montezuma giving a royal welcome to Cortés.

RIGHT: Aztecs greeting Columbus and his fleet with welcoming gifts as he lands on Guanaja.

possessors from avarice, since it cannot be hoarded or hidden underground". It is presumed that he was referring to the fact that the beans could not be stored for long without rotting.

The writings of Thomas Gage, a seventeenth-century English Dominican friar, are a rich source of information on chocolate. Visiting the City of Mexico, Gage describes how the cacao bean is used as "both meat and current money". Basing the exchange rate on the Spanish real, which at that time (1625) was worth sixpence (2½p), he explained that two hundred small cacao beans were worth one Spanish real, and "with these the Indians buy what they list, for five, nay for two cacaos, which is a very small part of a real, they do buy fruits and the like".

THE CACAO PLANTATIONS

When Cortés set out on his voyage to the New World, his primary goal was to find El Dorado – Aztec gold. When he failed to unearth the dreamed-of riches, his attention turned to cacao beans. Having seen them used as currency, and noticing the importance attached to them, Cortés soon realized that money could literally be made to grow on trees. He devoted the next few years to exploiting the commercial potential of this "liquid gold" by setting up cacao plantations around the Caribbean.

Cacao was cheap to cultivate and reasonably profitable, and the prospect of easy riches attracted plenty of Spanish colonists. Before long, the Spanish had established plantations in Mexico, Ecuador, Venezuela, Peru, and the islands of Jamaica and Hispaniola (now called Haiti and the Dominican Republic). Cacao production has since spread all over the world, but the plantations in these original regions still produce the most highly prized varieties of bean.

THE SPANISH SECRET

The Spanish colonists had tried to keep the secret of cultivating and preparing cacao to themselves, and with good reason – they were making fat profits out of processing the beans in Latin America before shipping them to Europe. However, the colonists did not remain in sole possession of their secret forever. In 1580, the first ever chocolate-processing plant was set up in Spain. From then on the popularity of chocolate gradually spread to other European countries.

LEFT: An early illustration showing cacao pods drying and a cacao tree growing under a shade-creating "mother" tree.

ABOVE: This lithograph, produced by the Empire Marketing Board, shows cacao pods being gathered.

These, in turn, established their own plantations, trade routes and processing facilities.

The Dutch transplanted the tree to their East Indian states of Java and Sumatra in the early seventeenth century, and from there it spread to the Philippines, New Guinea, Samoa and Indonesia with a degree of financial success made possible by the exploitation of hundreds of thousands of African slaves. The French settled in Martinique in 1660, and in Brazil in 1677, along with the Portuguese. Trinidad was fought over by the Dutch, the French and the British for years; it eventually went to the British in 1802. In the early nineteenth century, the Portuguese successfully transplanted Brazilian cacao saplings to the island of São Tomé off the African coast, and later to the island of Fernando Póo (now called Bioko) and West Africa. By the end of the nineteenth century, the Germans had settled in the Cameroons and the British in Sri Lanka. Plantations have since spread to South-East Asia, and Malaysia is now one of the world's leading producers.

> #### — CACAO FEVER —
>
> It was no easy job for the early planters to clear the jungle, but their fierce determination spurred them on. A Brazilian writer, Jorge Amado, described the vision of those early planters gripped by "cacao fever": "He does not see the forest ... choked with dense creepers and century-old trees, inhabited by wild animals and apparitions. He sees fields planted with cacao trees, straight rows of trees bearing golden fruit, ripe and yellow. He sees plantations pushing the forest back and stretching as far as the horizon."

THE POWER OF CHOCOLATE

To the Aztecs, chocolate was a source of spiritual wisdom, tremendous energy and enhanced sexual powers. The drink was highly prized as a nuptial aid, and, predictably, was the favourite beverage at wedding ceremonies. The Emperor Montezuma was reputed to get through fifty flagons of chocolate a day, always fortifying himself with a cup before entering his harem.

Although drunk on a daily basis, chocolate was still considered an exotic luxury and consumed primarily by kings, noblemen and the upper ranks of the priesthood. (Some historians say that priests would not have drunk chocolate, arguing that it would have been the equivalent of a priest quaffing champagne every day.)

Because of its renowned energy-boosting properties, chocolate was also given to Aztec warriors to fortify them on military campaigns. The chocolate was compressed into conveniently travel-sized tablets and wafers. Perhaps as a kind of incentive scheme a special law was instated declaring that unless a warrior went to war, he was forbidden to drink chocolate or eat luxury meats, or wear cotton, flowers or feathers – even if he was a royal prince or nobleman.

The Spanish colonists, too, became infatuated by the chocolate mystique. Once they had become accustomed to the strangeness of the drink, they took to it with enthusiasm. The Jesuit, José de Acosta, wrote "The Spaniards, both men and women, that are accustomed to the country, are very greedy of this chocolaté. They say they make diverse sortes of it, some hote, some colde, and put therein much of that chili".

Increasingly aware of its restorative values, Cortés convinced Carlos I of Spain of the enormous potential of this New World health food: "… the divine drink which builds up resistance and

fights fatigue. A cup of this precious drink enables a man to walk for a whole day without food".

Thomas Gage was heavily reliant on it too. He wrote: "Two or three hours after a good meal of three or four dishes of mutton, veal or beef, kid, turkeys or other fowles, our stomackes would bee ready to faint, and so wee were fain to support them with a cup of chocolatte".

RITES, RITUALS AND CEREMONIES

The writings of New World travellers give us fascinating insights into the strange and sometimes barbaric rites, rituals and ceremonies attached to the cacao bean and the drinking of chocolate.

Religious rituals took place at different stages during cultivation. The Maya always held a planting festival in honour of the gods during which they sacrificed a dog with a cacao-coloured spot in its hair. Another practice, calling for a certain amount of commitment, required the planters to remain celibate for thirteen nights. They were allowed to return to their wives on the fourteenth night, and then the beans were sown. Another somewhat gory planting ceremony involved placing the seeds in small

LEFT: Chocolate was drunk by Aztec warriors in military campaigns, but it didn't win them victory over the Spanish.

RIGHT: An Aztec with his chocolate pot and molinillo. *The* molinillo *has shaped paddles for making the drink frothy.*

— *CHOCOLATE AND CUISINE* —

Contrary to what some cookery writers would have us believe, the Aztecs did not use chocolate as an ingredient in cooking. To do so would have been considered sacrilegious – rather like devout Christians using communion wine to make gravy. What possibly causes confusion is a classic Mexican recipe called *Mole Poblano,* turkey or chicken in a chilli sauce flavoured with chocolate. The recipe is often assumed to have Aztec origins, but the ingredients include several items – onions, tomatoes and garlic, for instance – that would not have been available then. This is a recipe for Mole Poblano:

8 dried mulato chillies; 4 dried ancho chillies; 4 dried pasilla chillies; 2 dried chipotle chillies; 1 small turkey; 50g/2oz/ 4 tbsp lard (or vegetable oil); 60ml/4 tbsp sesame seeds; 115g/4oz/1 cup blanched almonds; 1 corn tortilla; 2 crushed garlic cloves; 1 chopped onion; ¼ tsp each of ground cloves; cinnamon and anise; 6 black peppercorns; 50g/2oz/⅓ cup raisins; 3 peeled tomatoes; 5ml/1 tsp salt; 50g/2oz/2 squares unsweetened chocolate; chicken or turkey stock

Arrange the dried chillies in a single layer in a roasting tin and soften in a hot oven for 2–3 minutes, taking care not to let them burn. Discard the stems and seeds and put the chillies in a bowl. Cover with barely boiling water. Leave to soak for 20–30 minutes.

Divide the turkey into portions. Heat the lard or oil in a heavy-based flameproof casserole and fry the turkey until golden brown. Using a slotted spoon, remove the turkey portions from the casserole and set aside.

Roast the sesame seeds and almonds in a dry frying pan over a medium heat until golden. Remove from the pan. Cut the tortilla into strips and heat in the pan until brittle.

Put the almonds, tortilla and all but 5ml/1 tsp sesame seeds into a food processor. Add the garlic, onion, spices, raisins, tomatoes and salt. Drain the chillies, reserving the soaking water, add them to the processor and purée until smooth, adding some of the chilli soaking water if necessary. Add this purée to the fat remaining in the casserole. Fry gently for about 5 minutes, stirring constantly.

Return the turkey to the casserole, with the chocolate and enough stock to just cover. Bring to the boil, then lower the heat, cover and simmer gently for 45–60 minutes until the turkey is tender and cooked through and the sauce has thickened. Garnish with the reserved sesame seeds and serve with rice and tortillas.

NOTE: If you have difficulty in finding Mexican dried chillies, use 115g/4oz fresh green chillies and 2 small dried red chillies, and do not preheat them in the oven. Simply remove the seeds, tear the chillies into shreds and soak as above.

LEFT: A Mexican metate *was used for grinding cacao beans to a paste.*

LEFT: A mosaic of Quetzalcoatl, the Toltec king and god who, according to legend, brought the cacao bean as a gift to human kind.

bowls before performing secret rites in the presence of an idol. Blood was then drawn from different parts of the human body and used to anoint the idol. Other practices include sprinkling "the blood of slain fowls" over the land to be sown. There were also tales of frenzied dancing, orgiastic rituals and bloody sacrifices. The sixteenth-century Italian historian and traveller, Girolamo Benzoni, recorded that during festivals "they used to spend all the day and half the night in dancing with only cacao for nourishment". Another legend tells of how, as a prize, the winner of a type of ball game would be offered as a sacrifice. The unfortunate man was first fed vast quantities of chocolate in order "to colour his blood" before his heart was cut out and presented to the gods, who, it was believed, would be honoured by the chocolate-rich blood.

Another use of chocolate was as a face paint with which the Aztecs adorned themselves in religious ceremonies. Even the early Spanish planters believed that secret rites were necessary for a successful crop and performed planting ceremonies. From its earliest days, then, chocolate was regarded as a substance of power, a gift from the gods, a source of vitality and life.

BELOW: Cacao beans laid out to dry on plantain leaves.

FROM BEAN TO BEVERAGE

ABOVE: A seventeenth-century lithograph showing an imaginary scene on a plantation, with Aztecs harvesting, preparing and cooking chocolate.

The Aztec drink bore little resemblance to the deliciously smooth, rich and creamy beverage we know today; it was bitter, greasy and served cold. Early travellers give differing accounts of how it was made. Giramolo Benzoni, a sixteenth-century Italian botanist, described the method used in rural areas: "They take as many fruits as they need and put them in an earthenware pot and dry them over the fire. Then they break them between two stones and reduce them to flour just as they do when they make bread. They then transfer this flour into vessels made of gourd halves …, moisten the flour gradually with water, often adding their 'long pepper' [chilli]."

Still on the subject of ingredients, Thomas Gage described additions other than chilli: "But the meaner set of people, as Blackamoors and Indians, commonly put nothing in it, but Cacao, Achiotte, Maize, and a few Chillies with a little Aniseed". Maize was used to blot up the cacao butter which floated to the top, and also to bind and thicken the drink.

It seems that the grinding stone, or *metate*, was an important part of the production process. One writer describes the process in some detail: "For this purpose they have a broad, smooth stone, well polished and glazed very hard, and being made fit in all respects for their use, they grind the cacaos thereon very small, and when they have so done, they have another broad stone ready, under which they keep a gentle fire". Because of the crude manual processing, all sorts of undesirable bits and pieces – shells, husks and pith – were allowed to remain in the resulting

RIGHT: Aztec chocolate-making equipment: chocolate pot, drinking goblet, whisk and rolling pin.

liquor. In Benzoni's opinion: "This mixture looks more fit for the pigs than like a beverage for human beings".

A FROTHY BREW

The Jesuit José de Acosta wrote: "The chief use of this cacao is in a drincke which they call chocolaté, whereof they make great account, foolishly and without reason: for it is loathsome to such as are not acquainted with it, having a skumme or frothe that is very unpleasant to taste, if they be not well conceited thereof."

For the Maya and Aztecs the froth was an all-important and most delicious part of the drink. One historian pointed out the importance "of opening the mouth wide, in order to facilitate deglutition, that the foam may dissolve gradually and descend imperceptibly, as it were, into the stomach". The Maya made the drink frothy by pouring it from one bowl to another from a height. Later, the Aztecs invented a device that the Spanish called a *molinillo* – a wooden swizzle stick with specially shaped paddles at one end, which fitted into the hole in the lid of the chocolate pot.

The eighteenth-century missionary, Father Jean-Baptiste Labat, described this indispensable item in one of his books: "A stick is about ten inches longer than the chocolate pot, thus enabling it to be freely twirled between the palms of the hand." The *molinillo* is still in use today and can be found in Latin American shops and markets. The design of the basic wooden stick remains unchanged, but there are also beautiful antique pots and swizzle sticks in silver and other decorative materials, which have become collectors' items.

There is evidence of yet more ingredients than those

— *CHAMPURRADO (CHOCOLATE ATOLE)* —

The addition of maize would have turned the Aztec drink into a thin gruel or porridge known as *atole*. This is a type of fortified drink, not necessarily flavoured with chocolate, still served at meals or used as a pick-me-up by workers in the fields in Latin America today. The chocolate-flavoured version is always referred to as *champurrado*, from *champurrar*, meaning to mix one drink with another:

Put 65g / 2½oz / ½ cup masa harina (treated maize flour) or finely ground tortillas in a large pan with 750ml / 1¼ pints / 3 cups water. Stir over low heat until thickened. Remove from the heat and stir in 175g / 6oz / 1 cup soft light brown sugar (or to taste), and 750ml / 1¼ pints / 3 cups milk. Grate three 25g / 1oz squares unsweetened chocolate and add to the pan. Beat well with a molinillo and serve steaming hot.

mentioned by Thomas Gage. The Spanish historian, Sahagún, describing a menu of chocolate drinks to be served to lords, tells us that there were "ruddy cacao; brilliant red cacao; orange cacao; black cacao; and white cacao". Many of the very early recipes for chocolate share common ingredients, and from these we can tell that the likely flavourings for the lords' impressive choice of cacao were chilli, allspice, cloves, vanilla, a type of black pepper, various flower petals, nuts and annatto.

BELOW: A modern chocolate pot, whisk and chocolate from Colombia. The design of the whisk has not changed since the days of the Aztecs.

ABOVE: Aztecs poured chocolate from a height to make it frothy.

Sugar was not added until much later. There is a story that the nuns of Oaxaca, an Aztec town occupied by the Spanish until 1522, developed new recipes in deference to the Spanish sweet tooth. They added sugar and sweet spices such as cinnamon and aniseed, and so the bitter beverage of the Aztecs began its transformation to the delicious drink that we know today.

THE SPANISH VERSION

In 1701 an Englishman travelling in Spain gave a detailed and lengthy account of the manufacturing process developed by the Spanish. After the preliminary roasting, dehusking and grinding, the cacao mass was ground again to a fine paste with plenty of sugar, cinnamon, vanilla, musk and annatto. The chocolate was formed into blocks, along the lines of modern block chocolate, but even so, these were still used only for making the beverage, rather than as confectionery.

As far as we know, this is the recipe that was used throughout Spain and the rest of Europe until the process was revolutionized in the nineteenth century by the technological achievements of the Dutchman Van Houten.

FROM BEVERAGE TO CONFECTIONERY

ABOVE: *A 1893 poster with a background of cacao pods and leaves.*

VAN HOUTEN'S PRESS

In its early days chocolate was an extremely rich beverage. It contained a fatty substance known as cacao butter, which tended to rise to the top, where it would float in unappetizing greasy pools. Manufacturers overcame this to some extent by adding starchy substances to absorb the fat – a process similar to the Aztec tradition of adding ground maize.

Manufacturers had also tried unsuccessfully for years to devise a way of separating out the greasy cacao butter. Breakthrough came in 1828 when, after years of trial and error, a Dutch chemist named Coenraad Van Houten patented a new and extremely efficient hydraulic press. His machine was able to extract about fifty per cent of the cacao butter present in the "liquor" (the paste produced after grinding the beans), leaving behind a refined, brittle, cake-like residue that could then be pulverized to a fine powder.

Not satisfied, Van Houten went one step further. He treated the powder with alkaline salts in order to improve the ease with which it could be mixed with water. The process, which came to be known as "Dutching", also darkened the colour of the chocolate and lightened the flavour – a curious anomaly since plain chocolate is usually assumed to have a stronger flavour. Today many people believe they prefer Dutch chocolate because of its strong flavour, but it may simply be the colour that attracts them.

Van Houten's inexhaustible patience revolutionized the chocolate industry. It led to the manufacture of what we now know as cocoa powder, which in Van Houten's time was called "cocoa essence". It also led to an all-round improvement within the industry. Van Houten sold his rights ten years after he took out the patent, and the machine came into general use. Among the first customers were the Frys and the Cadburys, ever eager to outdo

RIGHT: *Modern packaging based on the art nouveau style.*

ABOVE: *An early advertisement for Van Houten's cocoa powder – "the best liquid drinking chocolate".*

each other. Both firms were quick to enter the cocoa essence market, actively promoting the product's purity and ease of preparation. The old-style starch-based products were classified as adulterated, resulting in several fierce legal battles between rival firms. Van Houten's press also initiated the industry's next step in gearing up – the large-scale production of chocolate as confectionery.

EATING CHOCOLATE

Having separated out the butter from the bean, the industry was left with the question of what to do with it – it was certainly too good to waste. What happened was that somehow one of the cocoa manufacturers – and there are conflicting claims as to who was the first – hit upon the idea of melting the cacao butter and combining it with a blend of ground cacao beans and sugar. The resulting mixture was a smooth and malleable paste

ABOVE: A charming poster for Bovril's nourishing new chocolate bars, or cakes. The lettering on the box refers to them as "the perfect food".

that tolerated the added sugar without becoming gritty; the fat helped to dissolve it. The paste was also thin enough to be poured into a mould and cast, and it is from this concept that "eating chocolate" was developed.

The Fry family claim to have been the first to market the new product. Reflecting the current popularity of French-style products, they named the bars "Chocolat Délicieux à Manger" and exhibited them at a trade fair in Birmingham in 1849. The bars were an immediate success, and eating chocolate

RIGHT: Hershey's famous little Kisses were introduced in 1907.

caught on in a big way. Not to be outdone Cadburys introduced the first box of small individual chocolates, followed by a Valentine's Day presentation box. Other companies, such as Bovril, began producing eating chocolate, and the new confectionery was firmly established,

As a result of the new craze the price of cacao butter rocketed and, predictably, eating chocolate became an expensive sought-after product popular with society's élite. Meanwhile, cocoa was relegated to the masses.

The United States developed their version of chocolate bars a little later on. After experimenting with cream and chocolate – time and time again, the mixture scorched or failed to set – Milton Hershey's milk chocolate bars finally appeared on the market in 1900. His world famous Kisses followed in 1907. Over on the west coast, Ghirardelli was making use of new chocolate-moulding technology, and soon added chocolate bars to their

ABOVE: Modern packaging with old-fashioned appeal.

lines too. Specialist chocolate shops began to spring up all over the country and most towns had at least one well-respected establishment producing hand-made chocolates. The early chocolatiers were too small to import cacao beans or invest in expensive processing machinery. Instead, they bought industrial-sized blocks of coating chocolate from large companies such as Guittard and melted them down to use as "couverture" for their own hand-dipped fillings. Alice Bradley's 1917 *Candy Cook Book*, published in America, devoted a whole chapter to "Assorted Chocolates" with over sixty recipes for fillings. Bradley stated: "More than one

ABOVE: Ghirardelli's first chocolate bars were "full of toasted almonds".

hundred different chocolates may be found in the price lists of some manufacturers." The American chocolate industry got its biggest boost during the Second World War, when millions of chocolate bars were issued to the American armed forces in Europe. By this time both Ghirardelli and Hershey were well-equipped for the challenge of supplying them.

CHOCOLATE TRAVELS THE WORLD

During the sixteenth century chocolate began its journey into the countries of Europe as colonialists exploited their new world discoveries. Reaching Spain first, then following trade routes to Northern Europe and Great Britain, chocolate eventually made its way back across the Atlantic to North America.

SPAIN

It was probably through merchants and also through contact between New World convents and monasteries and their Spanish counterparts, that chocolate found its way to Spain.

Once the first commercial cargo of beans from Veracruz had been unloaded in 1585 and the official trade routes established, chocolate quickly became part of the Spanish way of life, especially among society's élite. However, a French noblewoman visiting Spain was unimpressed. She says of the drink: "They take it with so much pepper and so many spices, that it is impossible they don't burn themselves up." Nor was she impressed by their dental care and personal habits: "Their teeth are good, and would be white if they took care of them, but they neglect them. Besides the sugar and the chocolate which spoil them, they have the bad habit, men and women alike, of cleaning them with a toothpick, in whatever company they are."

Chocolaterías, chocolate houses, sprang up in cities all over the country, and it became the fashion to visit them in the afternoons to drink a cup of the foaming fragrant brew, accompanied by *picatoste,* fried bread, to dip in it. Today, the chocolate drinking habit remains strong in Spain, and there are still many *chocolaterías.* A traditional time to take the beverage is in the

RIGHT: The chambermaid model for "The Beautiful Chocolate Girl" married a wealthy aristocrat and so got to drink chocolate herself.

BELOW: This early eighteenth-century Spanish tiled panel shows gentlemen serving chocolate to their ladies.

The Spanish like their chocolate thick — so thick that a spoon will stand up in it, and it can almost be classified as a food rather than a drink. Cornflour is used as a thickener, or sometimes eggs, which practically turn the drink into chocolate mousse.

— SPANISH EGG CHOCOLATE —

In a double boiler, melt 50g/2oz/2 squares unsweetened chocolate in 475ml/16fl oz/2 cups milk until thick and smooth. Keep stirring and add 115g/4oz/½ cup sugar, pinch of salt, 10ml/2 tsp ground cinnamon and 5ml/1 tsp vanilla essence. Beat 1 egg in the bottom of a jug with a molinillo, pour over the hot chocolate mixture, whisk until frothy and serve immediately.

ABOVE: The pleasures of taking chocolate are captured in this seventeenth-century still life by Philippe Rousseau.

morning with freshly cooked *churros* (piped strips of deep-fried choux pastry), which replaced the *picatoste*.

In Spain, as in the rest of Europe, chocolate was always associated with stimulating foods such as spices, coffee and tea; it was a long while before chocolate was used as an ingredient for confectionery and desserts. Although its first use was as a beverage, chocolate was also a flavouring ingredient in savoury dishes. Both the Spanish and the Mexicans traditionally add chocolate to sauces for meat and game, and even fish.

THE NETHERLANDS

The Netherlands became part of the Spanish territories in the fourteenth century. Because of this, the Dutch were familiar with chocolate from an early stage.

The Dutch West India Company eventually defied the Spanish ban on foreign traders and started shipping cacao beans in bulk to Amsterdam during the seventeenth century. They then re-exported the beans in small lots to foreign buyers, as well as setting up their own processing plants in the Netherlands. Until the end of the eighteenth century, production was limited and chocolate was only seen in the homes of a few wealthy merchants and financiers.

ITALY

There are conflicting theories as to how and when chocolate reached Italy. Some historians believe it was around the middle of the sixteenth century when the exiled duke Emmanuel-Philibert returned to power, having experienced the delights of chocolate in Spain. The popular theory is that chocolate was imported by a Florentine merchant, Antonio Carletti, who discovered it while travelling the world in search of new products to sell. The most likely theory is that chocolate was brought in as a medicine through the convents and monasteries.

By the seventeenth century a growing number of chocolate companies had become established in northern Italy, particularly around the towns of Perugia and Turin. These companies in turn began to export their newly developed products to other European countries.

A collection of recipes by an eighteenth-century Italian priest shows the imagination of the Italians in their use of chocolate compared with other countries. Recipes included such dishes as: Liver dipped in chocolate and fried, Chocolate soup, Chocolate pudding with veal, marrow and candied fruit, and Chocolate polenta.

FRANCE

France was also quick to fall under chocolate's spell. As with Spain and Italy, there are conflicting theories about the circumstances surrounding its first appearance. Some say it was a result of networking between Spanish and French monasteries. Another theory states that chocolate entered France as a medicine. There is certainly some evidence from the French historian Bonaventure d'Argonne that the Cardinal of Lyons drank chocolate "to calm his spleen and appease his rage and foul temper", and that he may have "had the secret from

ABOVE: Cardinal Mazarin travelled with a chocolate-maker.

some Spanish monks who brought it to France". However, there is also no doubt that the trend was largely set by nobility and the royal court as it was in other European countries.

The most popular theory is that the drink made its first appearance in 1615 when Louis XIII married Anne of Austria, the young daughter of Philip II of Spain. The new queen loved her chocolate with a passion and introduced it to members of the court. There were plenty of devotees: the king's personal adviser, the formidable Cardinal Mazarin, absolutely refused to travel anywhere without his personal chocolate-maker; and later

BELOW: A tapestry depicting the marriage of María Teresa, the Spanish princess, to Louis XIV. Chocolate and the king were her only passions.

Marie Antoinette, also very fond of chocolate, created the prestigious "Charge of chocolate-maker of the Queen". Chocolate parties held by royalty, *chocolat du roi,* became a fashionable social ritual to which it was the ultimate in chic to be invited.

The many anecdotes include the story of the Spanish princess María Theresa, who married Louis XIV in 1660. She is said to have declared: "Chocolate and the King are my only passions." (Note the order.) The princess brought with her a Spanish maid, who prepared chocolate each morning for her queen. The ladies of the French court were intrigued by this new drink, especially as word had got round that it was an aphrodisiac. Chocolate sales in France apparently sky-rocketed around that time. Another often-repeated story about the princess is that her passion for chocolate was so excessive that she developed a horrendous complexion, and that her teeth were black and riddled with cavities.

Throughout France, chocolate never failed to evoke strong feelings. In 1664 learned academics praised its food value, presumably because of the fat content, but at the same time it was violently attacked by other writers, who accused those who drank it of moral depravity. Even Madame de Sévigné, a French courtesan and a great devotee of chocolate, turned against it for a while. In one of her letters to her daughter she wrote: "Chocolate is no longer for me what it was, fashion has led me astray, as it always does … it is the source of vapors and palpitations; it flatters you for a while, and then suddenly lights a continuous fever in you that leads to death … In the name of God, don't keep it up …" In another letter she told a horrendous tale of the Marquise de

ABOVE: Chocolate consumption was often depicted as being risqué.

Coëtlogon who "took so much chocolate during her pregnancy last year that she produced a small boy as black as the devil, who died". Eventually Madame de Sévigné regained her enthusiasm, and in a wonderful letter she neatly got round the issue of fasting and chocolate: "I took some chocolate night before last to digest my dinner, in order to have a good supper. I had some yesterday for sustenance so that I could fast until the evening. What I find most pleasant about chocolate is that it acts according to one's wishes."

SWITZERLAND

After the mid-seventeenth century, chocolate was making an appearance in all the principal cities of Europe. Although

ABOVE: The elegant refreshment room where chocolate was served at Confiserie Sprüngli in Zurich.

Switzerland was later to become a major producer of chocolate as confectionery, chocolate as a beverage was relatively late in arriving. It was first noticed in Zurich in 1697 after the Mayor had enjoyed drinking chocolate on a trip to Brussels. By the mid-eighteenth century, chocolate was more widely available and was often brought into the country by travelling Italian merchants, known as *cioccolatieri,* who sold it at fairs and markets.

GERMANY AND AUSTRIA

Like Switzerland, Germany was also relatively late to take up chocolate. For years the Germans regarded it as medicine, and it was sold only by apothecaries. But by the middle of the seventeenth century, chocolate had become accepted among fashionable society, although enthusiasm varied from city to city. Berliners still looked on it as an unpleasant tonic, but the drink was a hit in Dresden and in Leipzig, where the city's *glitterati*

took to drinking it at the fashionable Felsche café, one of the earliest German *schokoladestuben* (chocolate houses).

Among Germany's confirmed chocoholics were the famous poets Goethe (1749–1832) and Schiller (1759–1805). Goethe was reputed to have found the beverage a deep source of inspiration and drank it well into ripe old age. During his travels he often wrote to his wife asking her to send supplies from his favourite chocolate-maker, Riquet, in Leipzig.

Germany started producing its own chocolate on a large scale in 1756 when Prince Wilhelm von der Lippe erected a factory at Steinhude and brought over Portuguese workers especially skilled in the art of chocolate-making.

In Austria, Viennese aristocracy were quick to take up the new drink, especially after the Emperor Charles VI had moved his court and his chocolate from Madrid to Vienna in 1711. Since Austria did not impose such punishing taxes on chocolate as Germany, it was drunk not just by the aristocracy but also by lesser mortals who could afford it. There is a story of a German traveller in Vienna who was horrified to see someone as common as a tailor drinking a cup of best quality chocolate.

Both the Germans and the Austrians were accomplished pastry-cooks. Indeed, in the Austrian imperial court it seemed that the head pâtisserie chef was on a par with the most senior general. Like the Italians, the German and Austrian pastry-cooks took a while to start using chocolate as an ingredient in their baking rather than just as a beverage. It was worth the wait – their most wickedly delicious creations, the rich Black Forest Cake from Germany and the Viennese Sachertorte, are now celebrated forms of indulgence the world over.

BELOW: "Goethe in the Campagna" (1787) by German painter Johann Tischbein. Goethe was a lifelong drinker of chocolate.

The popularity of chocolate spawned a whole new industry for the famous china factories in both Austria and Germany, and in France too. At the beginning of the eighteenth century, European factories from Vienna to Berlin to Sèvres started producing the most exquisite chocolate services in porcelain; before that earthenware or metal, including gold and silver, were the materials used. As well as the traditionally shaped serving pots, the new range included elegant cups known as *trembleuse.* These new porcelain wares were specially designed to protect the aristocracy from the embarrassment of accidental spills. They featured double-handled cups which fitted into a holder or a very deep saucer.

ABOVE: The interior of a typical seventeenth-century London chocolate house – hotbeds of gossip, frequented by politicians and the literary set.

GREAT BRITAIN

In the sixteenth century, when the Spanish were shifting cacao as if there were no tomorrow, the British couldn't have cared less about it. Even the pirates who plagued the Spanish ports and shipping routes seemed unaware of its economic and cultural importance, for they showed no interest in the valuable cargo. Like their Dutch counterparts, they are reputed to have thrown boatloads of it overboard in disgust.

When chocolate finally arrived in Britain, it did so more or less simultaneously with two other stimulants, tea from Asia and coffee from Africa. Coffee was the first to catch on in British society – it was relatively cheaper – but chocolate soon followed.

Documentary evidence of the first chocolate house in London appeared in *The Public Advertiser* in 1657, followed two years later by a paragraph in *Needham's Mercurius Politicus* that drew attention to "an excellent West India drink, sold in Queen's-Head alley, in Bishopsgate-street, by a Frenchman".

The most famous establishment was White's Chocolate House, near St James's Palace, opened by an Italian immigrant. A rival establishment was The Cocoa Tree in St James's Street.

LEFT: Sacks of cacao beans from the tropics arriving at an English warehouse.

RIGHT: "A Cup of Chocolate" by Sir John Lavery. Drinking chocolate in the new chocolate houses was a fashionable pastime for ladies of society.

By chance rather than design the two establishments catered to different political loyalties – The Cocoa Tree was the favourite haunt of members of the Tory party, while the Whig aristocrats and the literary set frequented White's. White's was the inspiration for some of the scenes from William Hogarth's famous series of paintings *The Rake's Progress*.

For the wealthy upper classes, both the coffee and chocolate houses were *the* place to be seen. They were hotbeds of vicious gossip and political intrigue, as well as popular gambling venues where vast fortunes were won and lost. In 1675, Charles II tried in vain to have both types of establishment closed down on the grounds that politicians and businessmen were frequenting them too often and were in danger of neglecting their families. It is also possible that he was trying to suppress the kind of talk that could potentially lead to a rebellion similar to the one that caused his father's execution in 1649.

The diarist Samuel Pepys (1633–1703) was an ardent fan of chocolate, or "jocolatte", and a regular frequenter of the chocolate houses. One entry in his diary records a horrendous hangover the morning after the king's coronation: "Waked in the morning with my head in a sad taking through last night's drink, which I am very sorry for; so rose, and went with Mr Creed to drink our morning draught, which he did give me in Chocolate to settle my stomach."

In England, as in other countries, the government seized on chocolate as a potential source of revenue. Importers were

LEFT: Examples of early packaging for Domingo Ghirardelli's revolutionary instant cocoa powder.

obliged to pay a hefty duty on every sack of cacao beans brought into the country, and in 1660 a tax of 8d (about 3p) a gallon was imposed on all chocolate made and sold in England.

These penalties led to an inevitable increase in smuggling cacao beans, as well as adulteration of the chocolate, for which anything from brick dust to red lead was used. Brandon Head in *The Food of the Gods* refers to "the reprehensible practice (strongly condemned)" of padding out chocolate with husks and shells. He goes on: "To prevent this practice it was enacted in 1770 that the shells or husks should be seized or destroyed." Some of these husks did not go to waste, however. Head tells us: "From these a light, but not unpalatable, table decoction is still prepared in Ireland and elsewhere, under the designation of 'miserables'."

By the mid-1800s, the high levels of taxation had come down, thanks to the vast volume of imports, as well as the influence of respected Quaker industrialists who had convinced the government of chocolate's nourishing virtues. Chocolate was now affordable by all and had become big business.

UNITED STATES OF AMERICA

The first chocolate found its way back across the Atlantic to North America around 1765, probably in the pockets of high-ranking English officials going to their posts in the east coast colonies. We also know that Domingo Ghirardelli, an Italian confectioner then trading in Lima in Peru, exported cacao beans and other essential commodities from South America to San Francisco to supply the needs of the gold rush hordes. Another possible route for cacao beans was directly from Jamaica after the Spanish had given up control there.

Thomas Jefferson (1743–1826), third president of the United States, is quoted as saying: "The superiority of chocolate, both for health and nourishment, will soon give it the preference over tea and coffee in America which it has in Spain." Because of the pioneering nature of North American society, chocolate was

given a somewhat different reception to the one it had received in Europe. Although the wealthy east coast society enjoyed chocolate, they drank it at home – chocolate houses did not exist. Another difference was that chocolate was generally marketed to the masses rather than the elite (as in Europe), with the emphasis on wholesomeness rather than sophistication, so it consequently reached a far broader segment of society than it had in Spain, France and England.

The first chocolate factory was set up in 1765 in Massachusetts by Dr James Baker and John Hannon. The Walter Baker Company was established in 1780 by Baker's grandson and is still synonymous with quality chocolate. By 1884, Milton Hershey, of the Hershey Chocolate Company, was producing baking chocolate, cocoa and sweet chocolate coatings for his famous caramels; and by 1885, Domingo Ghirardelli had set up his California Chocolate Manufactory in San Francisco. Right from the start, chocolate was big business in North America.

BELOW: Nineteenth-century advertising poster for curious chocolate products from the Walter Baker Company.

CHOCOLATE AND THE CHURCH

The Church played an important role, directly and indirectly, in the early history of chocolate. The bitter and bloody religious wars raging between Catholics and Protestants in the sixteenth and seventeenth centuries, were, in a way, the cause of chocolate's appearance and gradual dispersal through Europe. The Jesuits, actively involved in the religious wars and fiercely committed to empowering the Catholic Church, were a driving political force both in Europe and Latin America. It was almost certainly the Jesuit missionaries, rather than New World explorers, who were responsible for bringing the first chocolate into Spain, Italy and France; it would have passed through an international network of monasteries and convents. It was also thanks to the pressure of Jesuit missionaries that raw, rather than processed, cacao beans were eventually shipped to Europe. Before this, the Spanish colonists had had a monopoly on processing the beans in Latin America, making fat profits by doing so.

In Italy, the religious wars resulted in a great many high-level marriages between aristocratic families and the ruling powers.

ABOVE: Friar Drinking Chocolate *by Jose M. Oropeza.*

Until its unification in 1879, Italy was a collection of self-governing states, and it was felt that marriages of this kind were the best way of cementing diplomatic relationships and consolidating the states' collective power. The aristocratic brides liked to take their maids, cooks and favourite foods with them when they moved from one Italian state or foreign country to another, and so through them chocolate began to appear in all sorts of places.

Until the eighteenth century, chocolate was made by monks and nuns, both in Europe and Latin America, using the methods handed down from the Aztecs. Thomas Gage, in his book *The English-American, His Travail by Sea and Land, or a New Survey of the West Indies* (published 1648), wrote of "cloister churches" run by nuns and friars. He said these were "talked off far and near, not for their religious practices, but for their skill in making drinkes which are used in those parts, the one called

BELOW: Part of Columbus's mission was to conquer new lands in the name of the Catholic Church. This picture illustrates that religious fervour.

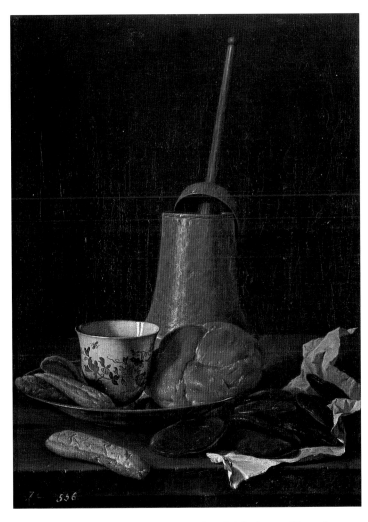

ABOVE: This seventeenth-century Spanish still-life shows tablets of chocolate, which were often made by monks and nuns.

chocolatte, another atolle. Chocolatte is (also) made up in boxes, and sent not only to Mexico, but much of it yearly transported into Spain".

In the New World, the Church generally took a pragmatic view of chocolate. It was popular with nuns and monks because it sustained them through the lengthy fasts they had to endure, and they were convinced of its health-promoting properties. There was an occasional difference of opinion in the Old World, however. A Spanish monk was said to have declared the drink diabolical, claiming its invigorating properties were the work of evil spirits, but his views went unheard. In 1650 the Society of Jesus (the Jesuit school) issued an act outlawing the drink to Jesuits, but this was impossible to enforce, especially when students started to abandon the school because of it.

THE CHOCOLATE OF CHIAPA

One major objection to chocolate appears to have been raised by the Bishop of Chiapa whose Mass was continually disturbed by its use. A famous and rather lengthy story told by Thomas Gage is worth repeating. The upper-class white ladies of Chiapa Real claimed "much weakness and squeamishness of stomacke, which they say is so great that they are not able to continue in church … unless they drinke a cup of hot chocolatte …. For this purpose it was much used by them to make their maids bring them to church … a cup of chocolatte, which could not be done to all without a great confusion and interrupting both mass and sermon".

Driven to distraction by the endless disturbances, the Bishop posted a notice stating that anyone who ate or drank in church would be excommunicated. The scornful women carried on their chocolate drinking regardless, and eventually the situation exploded into an uproar in which swords were drawn against the priests as they tried to remove the cups of chocolate from the women's maids.

The women retaliated by refusing to attend the Bishop's services, and attending Mass at the convents instead. The local priest warned the Bishop that if the women "cannot have their wills, they will surely work revenge either by chocolate or conserves, or some fair present, which shall surely carry death along with it!" Lo and behold, the Bishop fell ill and died a most unpleasant death eight days later. Gage wrote: "His head and face, did so swell that the least touch upon any part of him caused the skin to break and cast out white matter, which had corrupted and overflown all his body." Rumour had it that a gentlewoman "noted to be somewhat too familiar with one of the Bishop's pages" had persuaded the innocent young man to administer a cup of poisoned chocolate to "him who so rigorously had forbidden chocolate to be drunk in Church". A popular proverb in the region thereafter was "Beware of the chocolate of Chiapa".

DANGEROUS STIMULANTS

At the time that chocolate was becoming all the rage in Europe, there was a similar rise in the consumption of other tropical commodities such as coffee, tea, tobacco, rum and sugar; it seems that the Europeans were developing a taste for stimulants. The Church took a strong position and, with the exception of sugar, denounced the new foods as potentially dangerous. Even so, there was a certain amount of rule-bending when it came to chocolate.

RIGHT: Detail from a diorama based on a seventeenth-century engraving of monks drinking chocolate.

CHOCOLATE AS MEDICINE

Chocolate was used therapeutically as long ago as the fourth century, when the Maya first started cultivating the cacao tree. Sorcerers, the predecessors of priests and doctors, prescribed cacao both as a stimulant and as a soothing balm. Warriors took it as an energy-boosting drink, and cacao butter was used as a dressing for wounds.

ABOVE: Utensils needed "to make cocoa to perfection".

Later on, the Aztecs prescribed a potion of cacao mixed with the ground exhumed bones of their ancestors as a cure for diarrhoea. The Spanish colonists, too, were aware of cacao's healing properties. A traveller reported of his countrymen: "They make paste thereof, the which they say is good for the stomacke, and against the catarre."

However, chocolate was given a mixed reception by the scientific and medical community, who were just as vociferous as the Church when it came to debating the rights and wrongs of this mysterious new substance. In the sixteenth century, when medicine was in its infancy, many of the theories were based on the principle of "hot" and "cold" humours, or body energies, which, if not kept in balance, would cause illness. The Spanish classified chocolate as "cold" and tried to neutralize its effect by

BELOW: French doctors believed chocolate was beneficial for chronic illnesses and broken hearts.

drinking it hot, flavoured with "hot" spices. They found it hard to understand why the Aztecs drank unheated chocolate when it was already a "cold" food.

By the seventeenth century, chocolate had been given the seal of approval by several botanists and medical men, who discovered that it contained all kinds of beneficial substances. Henry Stubbe (1632–72), the English court physician, visited the West Indies to investigate the physical effects of chocolate. On his return, he published *The Indian Nectar,* in which he had nothing but praise for the beverage, with the proviso that adding too much sugar or spice was unwise.

Among the many others who sang the praises of chocolate was Stephani Blancardi (1650–1702), an Italian physician. He commented: "Chocolate is not only pleasant of taste, but it is also a veritable balm of the mouth, for the maintaining of all glands and humours in a good state of health. Thus it is, that all who drink it, possess a sweet breath."

The French faculty of medicine officially approved its use in 1661. The magistrate and gastronome, Brillat-Savarin (1755–1826), summed up in *Physiologie du Gout:* "Chocolate, when carefully prepared, is a wholesome and agreeable form of food … is very suitable for persons of great mental exertion, preachers, lawyers, and above all travellers … it agrees with the feeblest stomachs, has proved beneficial in cases of chronic illness and remains the last resource in the diseases of the pylorus." Some of his contemporaries claimed that chocolate cured tuberculosis. A French doctor, probably sensing chocolate's ability to lift the spirits, was convinced of its merits as an antidote to a broken heart. He wrote "Those who love, and are unfortunate enough to suffer from the most universal of all gallant illnesses, will find [in chocolate] the most enlightening consolation."

Praise was by no means universal. An eighteenth-century physician to the Tuscan court threw a spanner in the works by declaring that chocolate was "hot" and that it was madness to add "hot drugs" to it. He obviously noticed the effects of caffeine for he lists as ill effects incessant chatter, insomnia, irritability and hyperactivity in children. The French, too, became disenamoured for a short period, blaming chocolate for "vapours", palpitations, wind and constipation.

In general, however, the medicinal and nutritional benefits

— A MEXICAN RECIPE FOR LIP SALVE —

Take half a teaspoon [2.5ml] of cocoa butter from freshly roasted beans and mix to an ointment with sweet almond oil.

RIGHT: This eighteenth-century painting shows how chocolate was adopted by well-to-do households as a nutritious breakfast drink.

BELOW: This engraving from "Physiologie du Gout ou Méditations de Gastronomie Transcendante" (1848) depicts chocolate being served to uplift the spirits.

BELOW: This nineteenth-century advertisement shows British children enjoying cocoa. Medical experts in Britain proclaimed cocoa as "the drink par excellence for children, with whom it is a universal favourite".

of chocolate were well accepted. An early English writer described it as "incomparable as a family drink for breakfast or supper, when both tea and coffee are really out of place unless the latter is nearly all milk". Brillat-Savarin commented on digestion: "When you have breakfasted well and copiously, if you swallow a generous cup of good chocolate at the end of the meal, you will have digested everything perfectly three hours later."

By the 1800s charlatans were beginning to cash in on chocolate's seal of approval by the medical profession. Various forms of "medicinal" chocolate started to appear including sinister-sounding products such as "pectoral chocolate" made with Indian tapioca, recommended for people suffering from consumption, and "analeptic" chocolate made with a mysterious "Persian tonic".

By the end of the century, the genuine article was approved of by hospitals and sanatoria, as well as by the navy, the army and various public institutions.

THE FOUNDING FATHERS

ABOVE: Nineteenth-century British cocoa manufacturers were keen to wean the poor off their favourite tipple of gin.

GREAT BRITAIN

The manufacture of drinking chocolate in Britain was transformed by the Industrial Revolution and the cultural, social and economic changes that followed in its wake. During the eighteenth century the pioneering chocolate manufacturers were still using primitive manufacturing methods, similar to those used by the Aztecs. Technology gradually entered the scene with two key developments: a hydraulic grinding press, invented in 1728 by Walter Churchman, and, in 1765, James Watt's steam engine, which changed the food industry overnight. Another crucial development in chocolate manufacture was a revolutionary type of chocolate press invented in 1828 by a Dutch chemist, Coenraad Van Houten.

In 1853 the taxes on drinking chocolate were reduced because the volume of imports had grown enormously. By then the new railways had made transport easier, and power-driven machinery had largely replaced the old slow method of making chocolate by hand. These changes radically brought down the price, meaning that drinking chocolate could potentially be enjoyed by all.

It was during this era that several

RIGHT: Cadburys printed endorsements from the medical press on their packaging.

eminent Quaker families – the Frys, the Cadburys, the Rowntrees and the Terrys – became involved in chocolate manufacturing. These families established themselves as the main producers in Britain and succeeded in transforming chocolate from the drink of the aristocracy to the drink of the people.

It was undoubtedly the Quakers' evangelical outlook which was behind their decision to choose chocolate as a commercial venture. Because the beverage was so wholesome, the Quakers hoped it would provide a means of weaning the poor off beer and gin, their favourite tipples, and improving the quality of their lives in general. The Quakers were also concerned for their employees' welfare. They created exemplary working conditions and built model villages where education, healthcare and community services were provided for the workers, both active and retired, without charge. Cadbury's Bournville village near Birmingham and Rowntree in York are famous examples.

The Frys were the sole suppliers of chocolate to the navy, making them the largest chocolate manufacturer in the world. Not to be outdone, the rival Cadbury family gained the privileged title of purveyors of chocolate to Queen Victoria.

ITALY

The Italians have always been accomplished sweet-makers. They started using chocolate as an ingredient very early on and thus established themselves as leading experts in the art of making fine chocolates. In 1884, when the Russian Czar commissioned from the jeweller Fabergé his first golden egg with its surprise filling of precious stones, Italian producers introduced what may have been the first chocolate Easter eggs containing a surprise gift.

ABOVE: Military-style packaging.

The Italian chocolate industry is centred around Turin in Piedmont and Perugia in Umbria. Production on a commercial level developed in the early nineteenth century when Bozelli, an engineer from Genoa, designed a machine capable of producing over 300kg/660lb of chocolate per day. By the end of the century the industry was booming.

There are several long-established firms in northern Italy. These include Caffarel, from whom the Italians learned to make chocolate, and Baratti & Milano, from the Turin area; Perugina (now owned by Nestlé) from Perugia, makers of the famous "Baci" (kisses) chocolates with the memorable pack; and Majani in Bologna, who now produce the ultimate in designer chocolates.

SWITZERLAND

Unsurprisingly, Switzerland boasts an incredible list of founding fathers. The first, an enterprising young man named François Cailler, travelled to Turin in 1815, learned the tricks of the trade from Caffarel, then opened the first Swiss chocolate factory four years later. Next to set up was Philippe Suchard, inventor of the world's first chocolate mixing machine. In 1845 Richard Sprüngli opened his world-famous shop in Zurich, followed by a factory in 1900. Henri Nestlé, a chemist, invented a type of evaporated milk powder, which was used by Daniel Peter, a chocolate-maker, to produce the first milk chocolate bars in 1879. In the same year Rodolphe Lindt invented the "conching" process, which revolutionized forever the texture and flavour of solid chocolate bars. Richard Sprüngli's grandson, David, bought out Lindt in 1899; five generations later, Lindt-Sprüngli is Switzerland's largest independent chocolate manufacturer. Finally, in 1908 Jean Tobler produced the famous "Toblerone" bar, now marketed by Suchard. Its distinctive triangular shape was designed to represent the Swiss Alps.

FRANCE

The first chocolate factories appeared in the mid-seventeenth century, and, as in England, production was a slow and primitive process. Life became easier in 1732, when a Frenchman named Dubuisson invented a grinding table. This allowed the workers to grind the beans standing up, instead of kneeling in front of a floor-level stone, which they had done until then.

France's most famous mass producers were Auguste Poulain and Jean-Antoine Menier. Poulain set up shop in Blois in 1848, making chocolate in a back room. By 1878 he was producing chocolate by the ton from five different factories. In 1884 his son Albert developed a chocolate breakfast drink, now known as Grand Arôme and still loved by French children. Meanwhile, Menier, a pharmacist famous for his "medicinal powders", bought a small chocolate factory near the River Marne, intending simply to produce chocolate to coat his pills. When he died in 1853, his son Émile-Justin stepped in, concentrating on full-scale chocolate manufacture. A man of capitalist vision, Émile built a new factory in France, opened a factory in

LEFT: Menier cooking chocolate is widely used today.

RIGHT: As this 1893 poster shows, Menier chocolate has always been popular with French children.

LEFT: Established for over a hundred years, Weiss still produces quality drinking chocolate.

London, a warehouse in New York, bought cacao plantations in Nicaragua, and built a Bournville-like model village for his workers. When he died Émile's son, Henri, continued in the same expansionary spirit. In 1889 he arranged for electricity lines and telephones to be installed in the workers' homes, and, many years before the rest of the French working population, gave them the right to retire at sixty.

France's chocolatiers also include a strong contingent of smaller specialist firms that played an important role in forming the character of France's present-day chocolate industry. Debauve & Gallais was established in Paris in 1800 and are the oldest producers of hand-made chocolates in the city today. Another prestigious company is Weiss, based in Saint-Étienne for over a hundred years, and famous for its delicious drinking chocolate and hefty foil-wrapped chocolate drops.

ABOVE: The electronic automobile bought by Hershey in 1900.

UNITED STATES OF AMERICA
Chocolate arrived relatively late in North America, around the middle of the eighteenth century. The first industrial producers were Dr James Baker and his partner John Hannon, who built a chocolate factory in 1765 on the banks of the River Neponset in Massachusetts. In 1780 the company was renamed the Walter Baker Company, after John Hannon's grandson, and is still a household name today, producing baker's (a confusing generic term) chocolate as well as better quality varieties under their own name of Baker's.

Over a century later Milton Hershey, a successful caramel manufacturer from Pennsylvania, visited the 1893 Chicago World's Fair and was overwhelmingly impressed by German chocolate production machinery on display. With a shrewd sense of timing, he decided that chocolate was going to be a runaway success; and his company has never looked back. Milton sold his first milk chocolate bar in 1895, and since then Hershey Bars and Hershey Kisses have become part of the American way of life – just as he predicted.

Like his Quaker counterparts in Britain, Milton had a social conscience. He enlisted nutritionists to vouch for the sanctity of his product, set up a squeaky-clean working environment, and built the factory town of Hershey in Pennsylvania. The main thoroughfares are East Chocolate Avenue and Cocoa Avenue, while the tree-lined side streets are named after places where cacao is grown, or by types of bean – Java, Caracas, Arriba and so on. Milton went one better than the Quaker factory villages in England and provided very generous out-of-town facilities for his employees such as an amusement park, a zoo, sporting facilities and a theatre. Milton also made it clear that no "taverns, piggeries, glue, soap, candle, lamp-black factories" were allowed, making sure that his model working communities stayed as wholesome as possible.

It is interesting that the early North American and British manufacturers of a product that was, and still is, associated with sensory enjoyment and indulgence, should have had quite a puritanical outlook. A cynical view might be that their social philanthropy was a clever marketing ploy, but these businessmen did have a genuine social conscience, and it is perhaps another illustration that chocolate is all things to all people – both a luxurious treat and a wholesome daily food.

Milton Hershey was not the only American producer

pushing the wholesomeness of chocolate. Like-minded but rather more extreme companies included the Taylor brothers, who entered the market with their Natural Hygienist Practitioners, and Dr William Hay, of the still-popular Hay System of food-combining. Taylor's selling point was the curative, homeopathic nature of chocolate. This shows a continuity with the earliest European marketeers, who sold their chocolate through the apothecaries, monasteries and convents of the sixteenth and seventeenth centuries, and had much to say on the beneficial properties of the cacao bean and its products.

A much more colourful American chocolate producer was

ABOVE: Street signs to the main thoroughfares in Hershey.

BELOW: Early publicity for Taylor Brothers demonstrating their social conscience, while promoting the nourishing powers of chocolate.

ABOVE: A picture of the original Guittard building surrounded by scenes showing early chocolate manufacture.

Domingo Ghirardelli, an Italian confectioner with South American links who was originally in business in Lima, Peru. Ghirardelli befriended an American cabinetmaker named James Lick, who, in 1847 just before the discovery of gold at Sutter's Mill, moved from Lima to San Francisco, taking with him a large quantity of Ghirardelli's chocolate. Lured by reports of a lucrative market, Ghirardelli followed Lick to California. As astute and entrepreneurial as his fellow chocolate producers, both in

BELOW: The Ghirardelli company was the first in America to make easily dissolvable powdered cocoa.

the United States and worldwide, Ghirardelli foresaw the potential in satisfying the day-to-day needs of the goldrush pioneers, who by then were arriving in hordes. He set up a business in San Francisco importing and selling commodities such as sugar, coffee and, of course, chocolate.

There were various disasters over the years, including devastating bankruptcy and a serious fire, but business continued despite the inevitable setbacks in a volatile period of American history. By 1856 the company was known as Ghirardelli's California Chocolate Manufactory. The company was to make its mark on the chocolate industry in the 1860s when, by sheer accident, a way of making a low-fat powdered cocoa was discovered. The new product was known as Sweet Ground Chocolate and Cocoa and is still sold today.

The original factory buildings have become a well-known San Francisco landmark in Ghirardelli Square, and the company continues to flourish. It was bought by the Golden Grain Macaroni Company in 1963, which in turn was acquired as a subsidiary of the Quaker Oats Company in 1983.

Another chocolate maker, Etienne Guittard from France, set off for the gold fields of San Francisco in 1860. After three years, he hadn't found any gold, but the supply of fine chocolate he had brought with him to barter for prospecting gear had been enthusiastically received. The shopkeepers he traded with assured him that there was a future for him and his wonderful chocolate in San Francisco. Guittard went back to France, where he worked and saved to buy the equipment he would need. In 1868 he returned to San Francisco and opened the business that developed into one of the important American manufacturers of top-grade chocolate for wholesale customers. Some of the country's best confectioners, bakers and ice-cream makers (Baskin-Robbins, for one) use Guittard.

GHIRARDELLI'S ACCIDENT

Cacao beans have a high fat content and because of this do not combine easily with liquids when ground to a powder. Ghirardelli's most important contribution to the chocolate industry was the accidental discovery of a way of making a virtually fat-free powder.

A worker left some ground cacao beans hanging from a hook in a cloth bag overnight. By the morning, the floor was covered in cacao butter that had dripped from the bag. The ground chocolate left behind was almost fat-free and was found to combine with liquids much more smoothly. Ghirardelli's ever-popular Sweet Ground Chocolate and Cocoa was developed from this.

CULTIVATION AND PROCESSING

GROWING AND HARVESTING

ABOVE: Cacao tree and seedling.

There are many stages in the processing of chocolate, and there has been a corresponding amount of development in its history as it has grown from a cold drink to the complex and adaptable substance it is today. This chapter traces the most important steps in the production of chocolate.

GROWING

The cacao bean grows in large pods on the cacao tree, *Theobroma cacao,* an evergreen which thrives in tropical areas lying between 20° north and 20° south of the equator. The tree is an exacting specimen, for it refuses to grow where it is too high, too cold or too dry, and it demands shelter from wind and sun. It also needs protection from wild animals which delight in picking its pods, and it easily succumbs to various rots, wilts and fungal diseases.

It is traditional for the cacao tree to be grown under the protection of taller shade-creating trees, the conditions resembling its natural jungle habitat. In areas such as Grenada and parts of Jamaica, cacao trees grow successfully without additional shade, as long as there are sufficient moisture and nutrients in the soil. The cacao tree grows to about the size of an apple tree and starts

BELOW: A shady cacao plantation in the garden island of Grenada, where cacao production is a staple industry.

CACAO is essentially the botanical name and refers to the tree, the pods and, at one time, the unfermented beans from the pods. The term is now also used for beans that have been fermented.

COCOA refers to the manufactured powder sold for drinking or food manufacturing purposes.

bearing fruit in its third year. With luck, it will continue to do so until at least its twentieth year, and it is not unknown for a tree to live to be a hundred years old. The glossy dark green leaves, similar to those of the laurel, grow to nearly 30 cm/ 12 in long. The small pale pink flowers grow in dense clusters straight out of the trunk and main branches on little raised cushions, a feature technically known as "cauliflory".

After pollination, the flowers take about five months to develop into cacao pods. It's a colourful crop – the pods range from bright red, green, purple or yellow, changing hue as they ripen. Ripe pods are about 20 cm/8 in long, oval and pointed, each containing 20 to 40 beans, embedded in a soft white pulp.

HARVESTING

It is by assessing the colour of the pod and the sound it makes when tapped that the picker can be sure it is ready for picking. To be absolutely certain that the pod is ripe requires years of practice, and experienced pickers are highly valued.

The pods are removed from the tree by cutting through their stalks, those within reach with a cutlass, and those on higher branches with a curved knife fixed to a long pole. Cutting must be done with extreme care so as not to damage the "cauliflory", as this continually produces the flowers and therefore the fruit.

In some countries, harvesting takes place all year round, although most heavily from May to December. In other parts of the world, West Africa for instance, the main crop is harvested from September to February.

FERMENTING

The next stage is to split the pods with a cutlass, taking care not to damage the precious beans. These are scooped out, together with their surrounding pulp, and formed into a conical heap on a carefully arranged mat of banana leaves. When the heap is complete the leaves are folded over, and yet more of these giant

ABOVE: Early lithograph issued by the Empire Marketing Board in Britain showing cacao beans being scooped from the pods.

— TYPES OF CACAO BEAN —

There are two distinct species of cacao bean used in the manufacture of chocolate: the criollo (meaning "native") and the forastero (meaning "foreign").

The criollo, the Rolls Royce of beans and the most delicate, is in a way a "limited edition", representing only 10 to 15 per cent of the world's production. It is cultivated mainly in the countries where cacao originated, namely Nicaragua, Guatemala, Mexico, Venezuela and Colombia, as well as Trinidad, Jamaica and Grenada. The criollo's exceptional flavour and aroma are prized by chocolate manufacturers the world over. Not surprisingly, the bean is always used in combination with other varieties.

The much hardier and higher-yielding forastero bean is grown mainly in Brazil and Africa, and it accounts for about 80 per cent of the world's production. It has a stronger, more bitter flavour than the criollo and is mainly used for blending.

The one exception is the amenolado variety, known as the "Arriba" bean, grown in Ecuador. Its delicate flavour and fine aroma are considered equal to the world's best beans.

Finally, there are also several hybrid beans, of which the trinitario is the best known. As the name suggests, it began life in Trinidad where, following a hurricane in 1727 that all but destroyed the plantations, it was a result of cross-breeding. It has inherited the robustness of the forastero and the delicate flavour of the criollo, and it is used mainly for blending.

leaves are added to enclose the heap completely. This is the start of the fermentation process, which lasts for up to six days.

The chemical processes involved are complicated, but, basically, bacteria and yeasts present in the air multiply on the sugary pulp surrounding the beans, causing it to decompose to an acidic juice. The process raises the temperature of the heap and under these conditions magical changes take place within the bean itself. The colour changes from purple to chocolate brown and the familiar cacao smell begins to emerge – the first crucial stage in developing beans of superior quality. That said, the fermentation process is sometimes omitted, with planters and manufacturers arguing both for and against.

DRYING

After fermentation, the beans are spread out on bamboo mats or wooden drying floors. During the ten to twenty days needed for drying, the beans are regularly turned to keep them well aired and to prevent moulds forming. In some places, where rainfall and humidity are high, the beans are dried in commercial drying plants. However, the best quality cacao comes from beans that have been dried naturally in the warm tropical sun.

BELOW: The large and beautiful cacao pods grow directly from the tree branches and change colour as they ripen.

MODERN MANUFACTURING

ABOVE: A chocolate manufacturer inspects a shipment of beans.

CLEANING AND GRADING

Cacao beans arrive at a chocolate factory in the condition in which they leave the plantations in cacao-growing countries. They have been fermented and dried but are still a raw material with the edible part enclosed inside the hard skin, which is dusty with the remains of the dried pulp.

The beans are given a preliminary cleaning, during which any stones or other objects that may have arrived in the sacks are removed by sieving. The beans pass on a moving belt to storage hoppers, and from there they travel on another conveyor belt to the cleaning and grading machines. The beans are carefully inspected, and any shrivelled or double beans are discarded, as is any undesirable material still clinging to the beans. Next, the cleaned and graded beans are collected either in containers or passed on another continuous conveyor belt to the roasting machines.

ROASTING FOR FLAVOUR

Roasting is a crucial part of the process and serves several functions. First, it develops the flavour and aroma, and it enriches the colour. Roasting also dries the husk surrounding the "nib", or edible inner part of the bean, making its removal easier, and dries the nib itself so that it is ready for grinding.

The degree of roasting is extremely important. Overdoing

BELOW: The beans are cleaned and sifted through a mesh to get rid of small or shrivelled beans and foreign bodies.

ABOVE: A contemporaneous picture of Richard Sprüngli's famous factory, which opened in Switzerland in 1900.

it destroys the natural flavour of the bean and produces a bitter product, while under-roasting makes the removal of the husk more difficult and also fails to eradicate the natural bitterness of the raw bean. Some manufacturers who want their chocolate to have a strong flavour, but who are not prepared to increase the cacao content, attempt to achieve the required intensity by roasting the beans longer.

Different types of bean need different roasting temperatures, depending on their texture and flavour; the mild varieties are usually roasted at lower temperatures than the stronger types.

After roasting, the beans are cooled as quickly as possible to prevent further internal roasting.

BELOW: The beans are gently roasted to develop the aroma, enrich the colour and to dehydrate them prior to grinding.

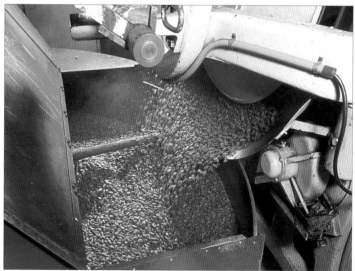

WINNOWING

During the next stage the beans are passed through the husking and winnowing machine, which cracks open the roasted beans, and blows the lighter husks away from the heavier pieces of nib.

Manufacturers send the husks off for recycling as garden mulch, or use them to make low-quality soft "shell" butter.

THE CRUCIAL BLEND

During the blending process, specified quantities of different varieties of cacao nibs are weighed and transferred to a cylindrical blender before they are fed into the grinding machines.

The blending of beans for cocoa powder is generally less exacting than for eating chocolate. The latter requires the utmost skill from the chocolatier since knowledge of the characteristic flavours imparted by different beans is only acquired by years of experience. There are subtle differences of flavour in each type of bean, and the final flavour is obtained by blending two, three or more types of bean after roasting. In the same way that the winemaker blends his grapes, the chocolatier needs to determine the proportion of strong and mild cacao beans necessary

ABOVE: A picture of the grinding hall in the Sprüngli factory. The rollers can be seen on the left.

to produce a blend that will result in a satisfying chocolate, and the formulae are jealously guarded secrets.

GRINDING

Once in the grinding mill, the nibs pass through a series of rollers, resulting in coarse particles that eventually turn into a warm paste because of the frictional heat of the grinding action. Then follows a second grinding to bring the particles down to the required size, usually between 25 and 50 microns (about 0.001in). Large particles result in coarse grainy chocolate, while very finely ground particles will produce a pasty and slightly sticky chocolate. After grinding, the cacao mass or "liquor" flows out of the machine into shallow metal containers.

THE PARTING OF THE WAYS

At this stage, further treatment of the liquor depends on whether it is to be made into cocoa powder or eating chocolate. For cocoa powder the next step is the extraction of a large proportion of the cacao butter. This is pressed out of the liquor, and the residue is formed into cakes, which go through one more grinding. Some cocoa is "dutched", which helps to make cocoa powder easier to mix with water. It also improves the colour and lightens the flavour. Sometimes a wetting agent is added, especially to the "instant" varieties of cocoa intended for use as a cold drink; it makes the powder easier to mix with cold water or milk. The wetting agent is usually lecithin, a vegetable fat found in egg yolks and soy beans. Chocolate destined for eating is treated very differently from cocoa powder.

RIGHT: Two types of instant drinking chocolate.

— BEAN BLENDS —

The final flavour of chocolate depends largely on the chocolatier's skill and experience in selecting and blending various types of beans. Availability of supplies and cost also have to be taken into account.

Types of cacao beans may be divided into strong and mild varieties:

STRONG VARIETIES	MILD VARIETIES
Accra	Caracas
St Lucia	Mauritius
Para	Sri Lanka
Trinidad	Arriba
Grenada	Java
Surinam	Madras
Cuba	Jamaica
Dominica	Seychelles

If made only with Accra beans, for example, chocolate will have a very strong, harsh flavour, whereas Caracas beans make mild but excellently flavoured chocolate. Superb chocolate can be made with a blend of 42 per cent Trinidad beans (strong), 21 per cent Accra beans (strong) and 37 per cent Caracas (mild).

THE MANUFACTURE OF EATING CHOCOLATE

ABOVE: Rolls of ground chocolate paste (foreground) are moulded into bars and various shapes in the moulding hall.

ABOVE: Prolonged conching transforms the chocolate paste into velvety smoothness.

MIXING

Cacao beans used for manufacturing eating chocolate are processed in a different way from beans used in cocoa manufacture. First, a carefully selected blend of roasted and ground nibs, the edible centre of the bean, is mixed with pulverized sugar and enriched with cacao butter, not necessarily extracted from the same batch of nibs. The mass producers in the chocolate industry are very keen on adding lecithin, a vegetable fat, to replace some or all of the cacao butter. This means they can sell the valuable butter at a profit.

The mixture then goes to the *mélangeur,* a round machine with a horizontal rotating base on which run heavy rollers. After mixing, the chocolate paste that is discharged from the *mélangeur* resembles well-kneaded dough.

When manufacturing milk chocolate, powdered milk or evaporated sweetened milk is added to the rest of the ingredients in the mixer.

REFINING

Next, the chocolate paste is ground between a series of five rollers, each succeeding roller rotating faster than the previous one. The paste enters the first pair of rollers as a thin film, which is then taken up by the next pair, through a carefully adjusted gap – rather like making pasta with a machine. By the time the paste emerges from the fifth roller it is wafer-thin.

As far as some mass-producers are concerned this is the end of the process, but the finest quality chocolate needs further treatment known as "conching".

CONCHING

The conching machine was invented in 1880 by the Swiss chocolatier, Rodolfe Lindt. The name comes from the French (*conche,* meaning "shell") and is derived from the shape of the machine, a large shell-shaped container.

The function of the machine is to agitate the liquid chocolate gently over a period that may be as long as seven days. It is a vital process in which the flavour of the chocolate is developed and mellowed, any residual bitterness is removed, and the texture reaches that essential stage of velvety smoothness.

Manufacturers of cheaper chocolate give as little as twelve hours to the process. Quality producers will continue conching for up to a week, sometimes adding extra cacao butter to make the chocolate smoother still.

During conching, various flavours are added, such as vanilla, cloves or cinnamon.

LEFT: Luscious slices of crystallized fruit are enrobed with smooth, dark chocolate.

Vanilla is almost always used and dates back to the days of the Aztecs. Our palates have become so accustomed to its flavour in chocolate that leaving it out would be like making bread without salt. Pure vanilla extract is used for the best quality chocolate, but cheaper varieties are likely to contain vanillin, a synthetic substitute.

TEMPERING

Once the conching stage is complete, the chocolate is fed into tempering kettles, where it is stirred and carefully cooled but still remains liquid. This is a tricky process since cacao butter contains various types of fat, all with different melting and setting points. If the chocolate mass is cooled too slowly, some fats will remain liquid and separate from the mass, creating a bloom on the surface when the chocolate finally solidifies. Tempering causes rapid cooling resulting in a more even distribution of the various fats.

After tempering, chocolate to be made into bars is pumped into moulding machines, while chocolate to be used as coating is pumped into enrobing machines.

BELOW: Hollow Easter eggs, filled with small chocolates, are a classic example of chocolate moulding.

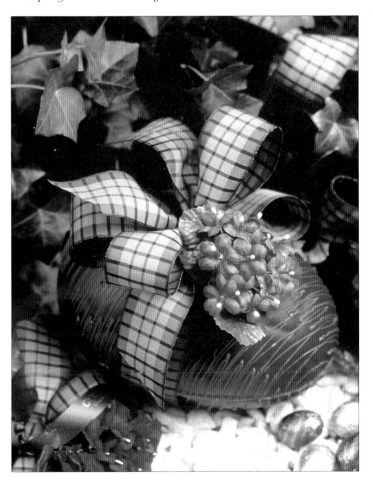

Mr R. Whymper in *Cocoa and Chocolate* (1921) told an interesting story of how, in the early 1900s, the popularity of milk chocolate "raised hopes in the breasts of manufacturers that a similar demand might be created among the masses for such articles as Date Chocolate, Egg Chocolate, Malt Chocolate". A number of patents were taken out, one of which was for mixing cacao beans and dates to a pulp, and covered the use of apples, pears and apricots for the same purpose. There was apparently a shortage of cane sugar at the time, and the fruit pulp was intended to be a sweetener.

Another patent was for "dietetic and laxative" chocolate. As Mr Whymper pointed out: "Such preparations must have only a very limited sale, so long as the chocolate-consuming public does not seek to find cures in its confections."

MOULDING

Liquid chocolate is also moulded into hollowed-out shapes which are sometimes filled with small chocolates. These products are often marketed as gifts for children, and specialist chocolate-makers give full rein to their creativity here, producing not simply exquisite Easter eggs, bunnies and hearts, but also pigs, fish, lions, hippos, crocodiles and

ABOVE: 1930's metal moulds for producing novelty chocolates.

cars. Because of the contact with the smooth tinned surfaces of the mould, good quality hollow chocolate has a high degree of gloss, which adds to its attraction.

ENROBING

Enrobing is the tricky process of coating confectionery centres. Liquid chocolate of a slightly "thin" consistency is pumped into the enrobing machine, where it is agitated once more and maintained at a temperature just high enough to keep it liquid. The centres themselves have to be warm when they enter the coating chamber, but not so warm that they lose their shape. The danger of a cold centre is that it is likely to expand when it comes in contact with the warm coating, resulting in burst chocolates. Enrobing is the process used not only for top quality chocolates in their luxury packaging, but also for the mass-produced candy bars that are bought as snacks around the world.

TASTE, QUALITY AND PRESENTATION

TYPES OF EATING CHOCOLATE

There is a wealth of wonderful chocolate products available, with an often confusing array of types, qualities, fillings and flavourings. Here is a brief guide on what you should look for and how to enjoy chocolate at its best.

PLAIN CHOCOLATE (ALSO KNOWN AS BITTERSWEET)

Plain or bittersweet chocolate must contain a minimum of 34 per cent cacao solids, but generally speaking, the higher the proportion the better the chocolate. Not so long ago, plain chocolate containing just 30 per cent cacao solids was considered high quality. Nowadays, as our taste and awareness of chocolate grows, 60 per cent is the preferred minimum, while for chocoholics 70-80 per cent is even more desirable. High quality dark chocolate contains a correspondingly small proportion of sugar. Adding sugar to chocolate has been compared with adding salt to food. You need just enough to enhance the flavour but not so much that the flavour is destroyed. Quality chocolate contains pure vanilla, an expensive flavouring sometimes called Bourbon Vanilla, extracted from a type of orchid grown in Madagascar. It also contains the minutest amount of lecithin, a harmless vegetable stabilizer. In unsweetened chocolate, which is found only in specialist shops, cacao solids are as high as 98 per cent.

ABOVE: Quality white, milk and dark chocolate.

COUVERTURE

This is high-quality chocolate in the professional league, used mainly for coating and in baking. Couverture usually has a minimum of 32 per cent cacao butter, which enables it to form a much thinner shell than ordinary chocolate.

LEFT: Couverture chocolate, which has a very high proportion of cacao solids.

RIGHT: Best quality couverture with a good sheen. Blocks of this size are supplied to chocolatiers.

— **FORMULA FOR QUALITY CHOCOLATE** —
56-70% cacao solids, to include 31% cacao butter
29-43% finely ground sugar
1% lecithin and pure vanilla extract

— **FORMULA FOR MASS-PRODUCED MILK CHOCOLATE** —
11% cacao solids
3% vegetable fat
20% milk solids
65% sugar
1% lecithin and synthetic vanillin

MILK CHOCOLATE

To some *aficionados,* milk chocolate is not really chocolate, but, increasingly, there are good brands around even though they may be difficult to find. A good brand will have a cacao solid content of around 40 per cent, but most mass-produced milk chocolate contains only 20 per cent. Mass-produced milk chocolate has a high sugar content, often up to 50 per cent. It can also contain up to 5 per cent vegetable fat, used as a substitute for expensive cacao butter, and artificial flavouring.

WHITE CHOCOLATE

This is basically cacao butter without any cacao solids, with some added sugar, flavouring and milk. White chocolate does not have the same depth of flavour as plain chocolate. It is mainly sold for its novelty value or to provide an attractive colour contrast

LEFT: A layered bar of plain, white and milk chocolate.

in chocolates and chocolate desserts. The best quality brands tend to be French and Swiss. British brands usually contain vegetable oil instead of cacao butter, as well as synthetic flavourings.

ASSESSING QUALITY

All our senses – sight, smell, sound, touch and taste – come into play when assessing the quality of plain chocolate. There are several points to watch out for:

APPEARANCE: The chocolate should be smooth, brilliantly shiny and pure mahogany-black in colour.

SMELL: The chocolate should not smell excessively sweet.

SOUND: The chocolate should be crisp and make a distinct "snap" when broken in two. If the chocolate splinters, it is too dry; if it resists breaking, it is too waxy.

TOUCH: Chocolate with a high cacao butter content should quickly start to melt when held in the hand – this is a good sign. In the mouth, it should feel ultra-smooth with no hint of graininess, and it should melt instantly.

TASTE: Chocolate contains a kaleidoscope of flavours and aromas which continue to develop in the mouth. The basic flavours are bitterness with a hint of acidity, sweetness with a suggestion of sourness, and just a touch of saltiness which helps release the aromas of cocoa, pineapple, banana, vanilla and cinnamon.

STORAGE

Humidity and heat are chocolate's greatest enemies; both can cause a "bloom" to appear on the surface. Heat-induced bloom

---

— TASTING TECHNIQUES —

It is best to taste chocolate on an empty stomach. If your chocolate is correctly stored, you will need to allow an hour or so for it to reach the recommended temperature of 19–25°C/66–77°F.

PLAIN CHOCOLATE: Allow the chocolate to sit in your mouth for a few moments to release its primary flavours and aromas. Then chew it five to ten times to release the secondary aromas. Let it rest lightly against the roof of your mouth so that you experience the full range of flavours. Finally, enjoy the lingering tastes in your mouth.

FILLED CHOCOLATE: Allow the chocolate to sit in your mouth for a few moments to release its primary flavours and aromas. Then chew it three to five times to mix the chocolate and the filling. Let the mixture melt slowly in your mouth so that you experience a new range of flavours. Enjoy the lingering tastes.

LEFT: The perfect bar of chocolate has a glossy sheen and a rich dark colour.

is the result of cacao butter crystals rising to the surface and recrystallizing. The flavour is unaffected but the appearance is spoiled.

Humidity-induced bloom is more damaging. It is a result of sugar crystals being drawn to the surface, where they dissolve in the moist atmosphere and eventually recrystallize to form an unpleasant grey coating. As the texture and taste of the chocolate deteriorate, too, the dustbin is the best place for chocolate that has suffered in this way. The ideal temperature for storage is 10–15°C (50–60°F), slightly warmer than the refrigerator, and the humidity should be 60–70 per cent. Chocolate also absorbs surrounding odours easily and should be kept in an airtight container.

BELOW: A bloom has formed on the surface of the chocolate on the right. An unaffected piece on the left shows the difference in appearance.

— WHAT TO DRINK WITH CHOCOLATE —

Generally speaking, chocolate and wine do not mix. The lingering intensity of the chocolate competes with the aroma of the wine, and chocolate's bitterness can mask the tannins essential to the wine's flavour. White wine or champagne drunk with chocolate is a particularly uneasy combination. At the end of a meal, coffee, perhaps accompanied by a fine cognac, whisky or bourbon, is the best choice. Professional chocolate tasters swear by a glass of cold, fresh water; as it not only quenches the thirst but also cleanses the palate.

Flavourings and Fillings

Every chocolate manufacturer has a secret condiment or blend of flavourings that he or she claims gives their product a unique character. Fillings and flavourings from the same tropical latitude as the cacao bean itself – vanilla, cinnamon, cardamom, coffee, rum, ginger, even pepper and chilli – are the ones most commonly used. Even in this age of "culinary fusion", when we happily mix and match cuisines in our never-ending quest for novelty, flavouring chocolate with spices from a more northerly latitude simply seems wrong – it is hard to imagine fennel or caraway-flavoured chocolate, for instance – but perhaps it is merely a matter of time before it happens.

Secret flavours

Every chocolate-consuming country has its favourite flavourings. Italy prefers its chocolate mixed with hazelnuts, almonds or chestnuts. France likes a nutty flavour too, but strongly flavoured dark bitter chocolate is also popular there. Spain likes spiced chocolate, and fillings such as almonds and dried fruits, America consumes mostly milk chocolate, often with whole peanuts or almonds embedded in it, while Britain

Left: Spanish chocolate packed with plump almonds.

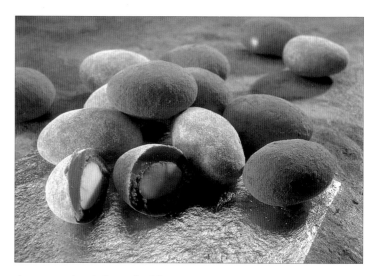

Above: Handmade "tartufini" from southern Italy – whole almonds coated in praline and dusted with dark cocoa and powdered sugar.

likes vanilla. Not only that, every country uses different blends of beans, and, as already mentioned, the subtle variations in the flavour of different bean varieties play their part in determining the final flavour of the chocolate. If we also take into account different processing methods used by individual factories, the number of flavour combinations is almost endless.

Within the scientific community, the complexity of chocolate's flavour is a source of enormous fascination to the flavour scientists who are regularly producing learned papers on the subject. Daniel Querici, speaking at the 1992 Oxford Symposium on Food & Cookery, summed up the subject of chocolate's flavour in a delightful way: "Its complex flavour profile looks like a royal peacock tail, although not fully deployed, as food scientists keep discovering new components."

Below: Plump and glistening, these unusual, luscious chocolate-covered figs come from Italy.

— Fillings —

Boiled: based on sugar and glucose and including caramels, butterscotch and fudge.

Creams and fondants: a mixture of sugar crystals in a sugar syrup, with fruit or other flavourings, coated with tempered chocolate.

Croquet (or brittle): molten sugar with crushed nuts.

Ganache: a mixture of chocolate, cream and butter, either rolled in cocoa powder to make a truffle or enrobed in tempered chocolate.

Gianduja: finely ground nuts and sugar mixed with plain or milk chocolate.

Marzipan: molten sugar mixed with ground almonds, coated with plain or milk chocolate.

Nougat: a mixture of beaten egg white, boiled sugar, nuts and/or candied fruit. Known as *Montélimar* in France (after the town where it is made), *torrone* in Italy, and *turrón* in Spain.

Praline: similar to *gianduja* but with a coarser texture and usually coated with plain or milk chocolate.

ABOVE: Italian chocolates with succulent fillings of walnuts, dried fruit and pistachio marzipan.

FANTASTIC FILLINGS

Chocolate has been used as a coating for anything from almonds and dried fruit to bizarre ingredients such as ants, and a look at the contents of a global box of chocolates will reveal many more.

In the United States, chillies and chocolate come together once more in the whacky confectionery range created by two chocolatiers from Oregon. Their products, which won an award at the Fiery Foods Show at Albuquerque, New Mexico, include Mexican Zingers, a creamy, green jalapeño salsa encased in a white chocolate shell, and Southwest Coyote Kickers, a red jalapeño salsa cream covered in light milk chocolate.

Although chilli-filled chocolates are legal in the United States, alcoholic fillings are not universally acceptable. As recently as 1986, only one American state permitted the manufacture of alcoholic chocolates, only eleven states permitted their sale, and

BELOW: Handmade British chocolates with melt-in-the-mouth fondant fillings, delicately flavoured with violet and rose.

even then the permitted alcohol levels were severely restricted.

Move on to Europe, however, and it is a different story. In Italy smooth dark chocolates are filled with decadent liqueur-soaked fruits – cherries, kumquats, slices of dried peach, pear, apricots and oranges. There are also plump prunes, dates and walnuts filled with marzipan and covered with dark chocolate.

In Britain, chocolate lovers can enjoy delicate fondant fillings such as violet and rose creams or marzipan; truffle fillings laced with champagne, Cointreau or Drambuie; or chunks of stem ginger, and whole Brazil nuts. France is the birthplace of the dusky chocolate truffle created in the late nineteenth century by the Duc de Praslin, one of Louis XIV's ministers. At that time it was considered amusing to create a food resembling something totally unrelated. *Truffes au chocolat* were deeply rich, buttery chocolate balls that were then rolled in dark cocoa powder to resemble the savoury black fungi from Périgord.

The dragée is a French confectionery classic that in its original form, almonds coated with sugar and honey, dates back to the thirteenth century. The dragée adapted well to the introduction of chocolate and now consists of praline or nuts covered in chocolate and a hard sugar coating.

CHOCOLATE WRAPPERS AND BOXES

Wrapping and packaging tell a great deal about what kind of chocolate is inside. Much can be learnt from the nutritional information on a bar, while the style of its presentation says much about who is expected to buy it.

WORDING ON WRAPPERS
As with the label on a bottle of fine wine or virgin olive oil, the wording on a chocolate wrapper can provide significant clues as to the quality of the product, so for a chocolate lover it is worth becoming familiar with the terminology.

An area of confusion arises over the terms "cacao liquor" and "cacao solids". Liquor is the term used in the United States, while Europe favours solids, but both refer to the same thing – the entire cacao content including the butter. This is usually expressed as a percentage of the net weight of the end product. Cacao content ranges from 15 per cent, which hardly comes into the category of chocolate, to an incredible 99 per cent, which is an almost inedible but interesting experience.

ABOVE: A wrapper that makes a feature of the high cacao content.

Since the setting up of the European Union, legislation on the labelling of food has become much more regulated, and the classification of chocolate has become an issue. Some chocolate-producing countries feel that Britain's product should be classified as "vegolate" because of its use of vegetable fat and low cacao content. Happily for British chocolate producers this has as yet remained a discussion point only.

WHAT TO LOOK FOR
The key indicator of quality is the cacao content – the combined total of cacao solids (liquor) and cacao butter. In some cases, couverture for instance, the cacao

LEFT: As well as listing the ingredients, some wrappers are packed with other interesting information.

butter content is itemized separately. In the case of plain chocolate, a minimum of 50 per cent total cacao is an indicator of quality. Quality milk chocolate should have a minimum of 30 per cent. Since sugar makes up the balance of the ingredients, a high sugar content is a warning of a correspondingly low cacao content.

Unlike wine labels, which mention the grape variety, chocolate wrappers rarely divulge the type of cacao bean used and are not obliged to do so. An exception is in France, where the words *fine cocoa* mean that the superior varieties of bean, such as the criollo, have been used.

Vegetable or animal fats are used as a cheap substitute for some or all of the cacao butter, so if either is listed as an ingredient, the chocolate is not going to come up to scratch. The fact that they are not listed, however, does not always necessarily mean they are not present. In Britain, for example, up to 5 per cent cacao butter substitutes can be included without mentioning them on the wrapper.

Lecithin, an emulsifier derived from egg yolk and soya beans, is used in all types of chocolate, and at 1 per cent or less is not an indicator of inferior quality. Its function is to stabilize the chocolate and to absorb any moisture.

As far as flavourings are concerned, look for the words "pure vanilla extract". If "vanillin", a synthetic substitute, or simply the word "flavouring" is listed, the chocolate is likely to be of inferior quality.

The Americans outdo any other nation in the world when it comes to providing information on the ingredients that go into their chocolate; the wrappers and packaging often read like a book. There are very precise

LEFT AND BELOW: Early chocolate boxes often featured inlaid metal decorations and intricate decorative painting.

LEFT: The ultimate in kitsch packaging, this opulent white plastic "grand piano" chocolate box comes from Germany.

— NATIONAL PREFERENCES —

According to the American writer, Nika Standen Hazelton, "Chocolate in a blue wrapper won't sell in Shanghai or Hong Kong because the Chinese associate blue with death. Neither Swiss nor Germans like girl pictures on their chocolate packages, but want a realistic reproduction of the contents."

specifications for the quantity of cacao solids in different types of chocolate; all flavouring ingredients must be fully declared; there are additional lists of sugars, such as dextrose and glucose, which all have maximum permitted levels; and there is always a detailed panel of nutritional information.

CHOCOLATE BOXES

Chocolate-makers have been strongly aware of the value of shelf-appeal since the industry's early days. In France the most exquisitely designed chocolate boxes came into vogue as early as 1780, featuring beautiful paintings, intricately embossed plaques and inlaid semi-precious stones. Britain's chocolate boxes were not so ostentatious; they featured sentimental images that were very much the fashion when boxed chocolates came on

the market. The first was produced in 1868 by Cadbury and featured a painting of a young girl cuddling a kitten; the model was Richard Cadbury's daughter Jessica.

Also part of the appeal are the beautiful papers used to line boxes and separate layers of chocolate. Although grease-resistant, the types of paper used have always had a special quality. They may be elaborately padded or embossed with gold or silver, or mysteriously translucent, like crisp tracing paper, with a swirly hammered finish. Another type of paper is known as glasine. It has a waxy feel and comes in wonderfully glossy, dark colours, almost smelling of chocolate in its own right.

Nowadays, packaging design veers from one extreme of style to another. Reminiscent of the glamourous thirties, there are amazingly lavish fabric-covered boxes trimmed with satiny ribbons and roses. In the kitsch category there is a large, white grand-piano-shaped box from Germany with chocolates hidden beneath the lid, and at the other end of the spectrum there is the ultimate in modern minimalist designer chocolates and packaging with slim chocolates wrapped in gold leaf.

BELOW: The packaging room at Cadbury's factory in 1932. Cadbury were the first manufacturer in Britain to produce boxed chocolates.

BELOW: Espresso-infused dark chocolate truffle fingers from the United States, end-wrapped with delicate gold foil.

A WORLD OF CHOCOLATE

In the next few pages of the book we survey some of the world's highest quality chocolate products. This is not a comprehensive selection, and it includes some of the most familiar quality brands as well as the more exclusive. Some products, such as the famous Toblerone bars, are internationally popular and universally available, and others, such as the exquisite chocolates made by the small specialist companies in America, are known to a much smaller market, but their first-class products are available by mail order and their market will increase as our appreciation of chocolate becomes more discerning.

BELGIUM

Belgium is renowned for its *ballotins,* chocolate-covered pralines, invented by Jean Neuhaus who, in 1912, developed coating chocolate capable of containing liquid fillings. Today NEUHAUS is well known for its flavoured Côte d'Or bars.

Of all Belgian chocolate companies, GODIVA must be the most recognized internationally. Established in 1929 by the Drap family, the company has 14-year old Joseph Drap to thank for its success. Realising people needed a little luxury in the austere post-war years Joseph created the chocolate truffle. They were marketed under the name of Godiva and were an instant success. Belgium also boasts many smaller specialists producing their own excellent chocolates.

ABOVE: A selection of Kim's Cachet chocolates, exported worldwide.

CHARLEMAGNE produces superior quality thin squares of plain and white chocolate with exotic flavours such as spiced ginger, cardamom and coffee, and spiced Earl Grey tea.

KIM'S, established in 1987 and manufacturer of the widely available luxury Cachet brand, specializes in handmade fillings. Kim's range includes white, milk and plain chocolate bars with luscious cream fillings such as hazelnut, coconut truffle, mocha and vanilla.

PIERRE COLAS specializes in unusual bars of plain and milk chocolate that are set in antique moulds and flavoured with esoteric combinations of cardamom, juniper, pink peppercorns and lavender. The company supplies specialist retailers in Belgium, Spain, France and the London chocolate shop Rococo.

WITTAMER probably ranks highest with connoisseurs. The range includes unusual seasonal specialities and Wittamer's famous Samba cake made with two contrasting chocolate mousses.

THE NETHERLANDS

The Netherlands is the birthplace of Coenraad Van Houten who revolutionized the chocolate industry with his cocoa press. With this background, it is not surprising that the Dutch chocolate industry today concentrates largely on cocoa rather than eating chocolate. The four biggest companies, VAN HOUTEN, BENSDORP, DE ZAAN and GERKENS, were all set up in the nineteenth century and continue to supply the world with fine-quality unsweetened cocoa powder. Van Houten is now based in Germany, having undergone several takeovers

and mergers, and trades in Europe, the United States, Hong Kong and Singapore.

The Netherlands do produce a certain amount of eating chocolate, however, and enthusiasts enjoy Dutch chocolate for its dark colour and distinctive flavour. DROSTE, of the distinctive "Droste man" logotype, makes delicious chocolate discs, or pastilles, from which the logotype is derived. Bensdorp and Van Houten also make quality chocolate.

LEFT: Droste are famous for their chocolate pastilles.

GERMANY

The Germans are one of the largest consumers of chocolate in Europe. Faced with this demanding clientele, German chocolate manufacturers pride themselves on producing fresh, quality chocolates made with the very best ingredients.

CONFISERIE HEINEMANN, based in München-Gladbach and run by master chocolatier Heinz Heinemann, makes over sixty varieties of freshly made chocolates every day, including exceptional champagne truffles. Heinemann also offers an interesting range of moulded chocolate-filled seasonal specialities.

DREIMEISTER is a long-established family enterprise set up by the father of Hans Wilhelm Schröder, the present owner, and originally known as Café Schröder. Although the company has a large turnover and supplies to hotels, restaurants and airlines, Dreimeister produces the freshest of chocolates and truffles, made only with top-quality ingredients.

FEODORA is probably Germany's best-known brand

RIGHT: Leysieffer's freshly made seasonal chocolate.

Internationally. Their chocolate is wonderfully smooth due to lengthy conching. The elegantly packaged quality chocolates include champagne truffles, bitter milk chocolate wafers, espresso Brazil chocolates and luxury pralines.

HACHEZ, based in Bremen since 1890, makes chocolates exclusively with rare cacao beans from Venezuela and Ecuador. Loved by generations of chocolate connoisseurs, the range includes melt-in-the-mouth cat's tongues, gold-covered nut sticks, ginger sticks, chocolate leaves and fruit cream-filled chocolate pastilles.

LEYSIEFFER has produced handmade chocolates in its Osnabrück bakery since 1909. In order to guarantee absolute freshness, the company starts manufacture only on receipt of an order. Its products include good quality white and milk chocolate, flavoured with a tempting range of ingredients – cinnamon, ginger, orange, pistachio and a mouthwatering combination of mocca and Jamaica rum.

STOLLWERCK in Cologne began as a bakery in 1839 and is now an international group with impressive headquarters on the banks of the River Elbe. The Imhoff-Stollwerck Museum boasts a fascinating collection of chocolate-related exhibits, including a collection of vending machines resembling grandfather clocks, porcelain chocolate services and printed ephemera, as well as a tropical greenhouse planted with young cacao trees. The company produces a wide range of chocolates for all levels of the market.

BELOW: Feodora's elegant range produced for the international market.

AUSTRIA

Austria's chocolate delicacies include both pâtisserie and confectionery. World-famous pâtisserie establishments are the palatial HOTEL IMPERIAL, Vienna's grandest, and home of Imperial Torte, an unbelievably rich layered square chocolate cake; and the HOTEL SACHER, famous for its delectable Sachertorte, a moist apricot-glazed rich chocolate cake; and DEMEL, the celebrated Viennese pâtisserie, which produces a rival version of Sachertorte based on a recipe said to have been given to Anna Demel by Franz Sacher's son. Demel also

produces whole roasted cacao beans coated with fine chocolate.

ALTMANN & KÜHNE, established in Vienna for more than eighty years, produce exquisite hand-dipped miniature chocolates, appropriately called Liliputconfekte, in the most unusual shapes. The chocolates are beautifully packaged in miniature chests of drawers and treasure chests.

MIRABELL in Salzburg produces traditional Mozartkugeln, an Austrian speciality consisting of creamy marzipan and hazelnut-nougat balls with a delicate chocolate coating.

ITALY

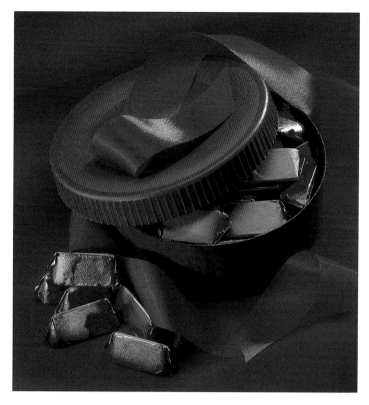

ABOVE: Gianduja *are Italy's favourite chocolate.*
RIGHT: *Italians prefer chocolate in bite-size pieces.*

Hazelnuts, chestnuts, almonds and honey have always been an integral part of Italian cuisine. It comes as no surprise therefore, that Italians like their chocolate nutty and sweet. They also like their chocolate small, so bars are often sold in single serving sizes – handy for a quick fix, should the need arise. Neapolitans, which look exactly like miniature chocolate bars, complete with individual wrappers, are well-known throughout Europe.

The Italians are creative chocolate-makers, and they excel at presentation too; Italian packaging is stunning, whether the design is traditionally ornate or 1990s minimalist.

CAFFAREL in Turin is one of Italy's oldest chocolate-makers. Established in 1826, the company purchased a chocolate-making machine designed by Bozelli, a Genoese engineer, and so became the pioneers in setting out on the route to industrialization. In 1865 Caffarel developed Italy's favourite confection, *gianduja,* a rectangle of luscious chocolate and hazelnut paste, instantly recognizable by its triangular profile and rounded ends. Nowadays most Italian chocolate-makers produce their own special version of *gianduja* using jealously guarded recipes. There is a glorious giant-sized version, *grangianduja,* as well as miniature *gianduiotti.*

An ancient culture of confectionery lives on in Italy's far south, and it was here in Salantino, in Italy's heel, that MAGLIO opened their factory in 1875. The business has passed from father to son and is now run by brothers Massimo and Maurizio. The Maglio range is based on plump, dark chocolates with inspirational fillings, including liqueur-infused dried kumquats, peaches, pears and oranges, marzipan-stuffed dates and prunes, and lemon-zest-coated figs stuffed with a whole almond.

Founded in 1796, MAJANI in Bologna is one of Italy's most creative chocolate-makers. Their specialities are *scorze,* deliciously bittersweet chocolate sticks still made to the same ancient recipe, and *"Fiat" Cremino,* launched in 1911 as a publicity stunt to celebrate the Fiat Tipo 4 car. The car has since gone out of production but *"Fiat" Cremino* live on. These stunning miniature squares are made with four types of layered chocolate, something like a brown striped liquorice allsort.

PERUGINA, based in the medieval city of Perugia, Umbria, was set up in 1907 by Francesco Buitoni, a descendant of the well-known pasta-making family. From humble beginnings making sugared almonds, Perugina is now one of Italy's largest chocolate manufacturers. The most popular brand in their extensive range is *Baci* (kisses), introduced in 1922 and still going strong. Lovers still like to discover the romantic messages hidden under the wrapper.

PEYRANO, an exclusive chocolatier in Turin, is almost unique in grinding their own cacao beans – very, very few chocolatiers do so. The chocolates are superb, especially their *gianduja.* Peyrano also sell *bicerin,* a very rare paste of bitter chocolate, cocoa, hazelnuts and honey used for sweetening coffee.

BELOW: Romantically packaged Baci conceal a lover's message.

SWITZERLAND

ABOVE: The Confiserie Sprüngli in Zurich, around 1895.

Three key developments undoubtedly contribute to Switzerland's national preference for its very delicate, melt-in-the-mouth milk chocolate. Switzerland is the birthplace of Rodolphe Lindt, inventor of the conching machine which transforms chocolate from a rough gritty paste to a state of silky-smooth perfection. Lindt also created soft, creamy fondant chocolate by adding cacao butter to the paste before conching. We have the Swiss to thank, too, for the invention of milk chocolate.

SPRÜNGLI in Zurich is one of the most famous chocolate establishments in the world. The shop in Bahnhofstrasse is renowned for its freshest of fresh *Truffes du Jour,* a heart-stopping mixture of finest chocolate, cream and butter, made to the highest possible standards. The company operates a worldwide delivery service which guarantees that the longed-for parcel will arrive within 24 hours of despatch.

Set up by master confectioner Rudolf Sprüngli in 1845, the company has been handed down through six generations of Sprünglis. When Rudolf retired, he divided his empire between his two sons. The younger, David, received the confectionery shops. The elder brother, Johann, became the owner of the chocolate factory. In the same year he retired, Rudolf Sprüngli also decided to purchase Rodolphe Lindt's chocolate factory in Berne. Overnight, the company acquired all Lindt's manufacturing secrets, and it was this transaction that was the foundation for the success of the now world-famous Lindt & Sprüngli company.

ABOVE: A 1935 street poster.

LINDT & SPRÜNGLI operates entirely independently from Sprüngli. The company produces an enormous range of excellent quality chocolates sold in supermarkets and specialist shops world-wide. One of their best products is the tastefully thin Excellence bar, a sublime blend of finest cacao beans with a hint of pure

ABOVE: Lindt's mini chocolate bars.

vanilla, and a cacao solid content of 70 per cent. This is closely followed in quality by Excellence Milk, possibly one of the best milk chocolate bars available. Another Lindt bar, called Swiss Bittersweet Chocolate, which is easily recognized by its traditional wrapper design, is also good.

SUCHARD in Berne is another long-established and respected company, now owned by the American multinational Philip Morris. Suchard was a gold medallist several times over at the 1855 Exposition Universelle in Paris, and their milk chocolate bar, Milka, produced in 1901, is well-known all over Europe. Since 1970, Suchard have been the manufacturer of the famous Toblerone bars, although these were originally produced by their inventor Jean Tobler. The bars were designed with a triangular profile representing the Swiss Alps. The name is derived from merging that of the inventor, Tobler, together with the word *torrone,* the Italian word for nougat. Toblerone is made with a blend of chocolate, nougat, almonds and egg white, and the bar is one of Switzerland's most popular products – outside the country at least. Enthusiasts can enjoy giant bars weighing more than 4kg/8.8lb, miniature bars and a whole range in between.

ABOVE: Bars of superior chocolate.

ABOVE: The famous Toblerone bars.

FRANCE

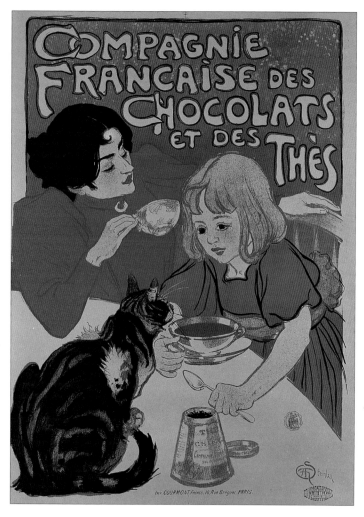

ABOVE: Early poster for the French Chocolate and Tea Company.

A large part of the French chocolate industry is made up of small, independent firms making ever more innovative *grand cru* chocolates to jealously guarded recipes. The French, who prefer dark, intensely flavoured chocolate, have a wide choice at their disposal.

BERNACHON, a greatly respected family of artisan chocolatiers, set up in 1955 in Lyon. Sharing the caring attitude of the

ABOVE: One of Bonnat's superb grand cru bars.

RIGHT: The ultimate dark chocolate.

Quakers, the company provides daily lunch for the workers and, until recently, housed them in dormitories above the workshop. The Bernachons travel the world in search of the rarest cacao beans and the best nuts and fruit. Their chocolates are the very best. The range includes unusually flavoured chocolate bars, truffles, pralines, *giandujas* and marzipans.

BONNAT in Voiron near Grenoble is one of the few companies that roasts its own beans. A purist at heart, master chocolatier Raymond Bonnat uses a single *grand cru* bean, rather than a blend, for each of the chocolates in his range. Bonnat's choice of seven *crus,* which consist of Côte d'Ivoire, Madagascar, Ceylon, Trinité, Chuao, Maragnan and Puerto Cabellois, is selected from the world's finest cacao plantations. Bonnat chocolates are available from specialist outlets in France, and from Mortimer and Bennett's shop in London, which is the sole British importer.

CLUIZEL, in Paris, is a family-run business set up in 1947, producing excellent chocolate with rare South American and African beans ground and roasted on the

ABOVE: Chocolate almonds.

premises. It is perhaps best known for a small and rather sinister chocolate bar containing 99 per cent cacao solids. Cluizel's chocolates are available throughout Europe.

CHRISTIAN CONSTANT, set up in 1970 in Paris, produces matchless ganache-filled chocolates. The flavourings read like an exotic travel brochure: Malabar cardamom, Yemeni jasmine, Chinese ginger and Tahitian vanilla.

The famous FAUCHON shop in Paris was established in 1925 by August Fauchon, whose passion was for collecting unusual merchandise. The company was taken over after his death by Joseph Pilosoff, whose granddaughter runs the business today. Fauchon specialities are the very best quality chocolate *marrons glacés,* truffles, pralines and ganaches, all exquisitely packaged.

LA MAISON DU CHOCOLAT in Paris was opened in 1977 by Robert Linxe, master chocolate-maker *extraordinaire.* Linxe's rigorous training and deep understanding of chocolate's complexities have played a major part in furthering the reputation of France's chocolate-makers. It was Linxe's collaboration with Valrhona which set the quality of their *grand cru* couvertures, which they in turn supply to smaller chocolate-makers. Linxe's specialities are exquisitely shaped squares, pyramids and lozenges of the very best plain and milk chocolate, filled with praline, buttery caramel or the lightest and creamiest ganache. The chocolates are sold in Paris and by leading specialist outlets in New York, Houston and Dallas.

LE ROUX, founded in 1977 in Quiberon, Brittany, is renowned for *Caramel au Beurre Salé* (salted butter caramel), and for rare chocolate truffles containing fragments of Périgord truffle.

MICHEL CHAUDUN set up shop in Paris in 1986. His award-winning work includes not only the highest quality chocolates but ambitious chocolate sculptures. Only the rarest cacao beans are used together with top quality fruit and nuts. His chocolates are available in Paris and Tokyo.

RICHART DESIGN ET CHOCOLAT started life in 1925 in the laboratory of Lyon-based master chocolatier Joseph Richart. Using

ABOVE: Elegant chocolates and packaging from Richart Design et Chocolat.

BELOW: A Chocolat Carpentier poster from 1895.

only the finest cacao beans, Richart produces exquisite, smoother than smooth, miniature chocolate squares silk-screened with designs in cacao butter. Fillings and flavourings are equally inspired. The choice includes pure malt Scotch, green tea, blackcurrants, pineapple, clementines, the very best Andalucian almonds, chestnuts from the Ardèche, and pralines and ganaches flavoured with thyme, curry, bergamot, anise or nutmeg. Beautifully packaged in slim trays, Richart's chocolates are sold in boutiques in Paris, Lyon and New York.

VALRHONA, set up in 1922 and based in the Rhône valley, is the leading supplier of couverture chocolate for smaller chocolate-makers. The beans are all of superior quality and include guanaja, pur caraibe, manjari and jivara. Each shipment is tested by a panel of experts. Its products include *Carré,* small chocolate squares made from individual bean varieties, packed in beautiful tins; *BonBons de Chocolat,* individual chocolates packed in gift boxes with a guide recommending the order in which they should be eaten; and the well-known Valrhona bars in their distinctive black wrappers. The cacao content of the bars ranges from 71 per cent for *Noir Amer* (bitter) to a relatively high 40 per cent for *Le Lacté* (milk).

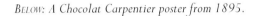

RIGHT: Valrhona Lacté has a high cacao content.

SPAIN

As recently as 1920, chocolate-makers in Spain were still using the curved granite metate for grinding cacao beans. The *chocolateros* would travel around with the *metate* strapped to their backs and bags of cacao beans under their arms. They would kneel on a little cushion in front of the stone and grind the beans in full public view so that the buyer could be sure he was getting unadulterated stone-ground chocolate. Nowadays chocolate-making in Spain is a fully industrialized process, but, even so, the tradition of quality craftsmanship is very much alive and well.

In some ways Spanish chocolate is indistinguishable from quality chocolate made in the rest of Europe. What sets it apart is the creativity and imagination of the chocolate-makers, and their use of the very best quality Mediterranean fruits and nuts. Spain grows some of the best nuts in the world, so there is no shortage of supply. Plump almonds, hazelnuts, pine kernels and mouth-puckeringly bitter Seville oranges are all used by the chocolate-makers with excellent results.

BLANXART, set up in 1954 in Barcelona, is one of Spain's smaller specialist firms, producing handmade high-quality chocolates from the very best cacao beans. The company prides itself on roasting and grinding the beans itself to achieve the desired perfection of flavour and aroma. The mouthwatering range includes a delicate curl of candied Seville orange dipped in bitter chocolate, clusters of chocolate-covered pine nuts, as well as liqueur-filled chocolates and several types of praline.

LUDOMAR, in Barcelona, specializes in superior, made-to-order chocolates, which they sell to pâtisserie shops in Spain, France, Germany and Britain. Specialities are plump, chocolate-smothered cherries; *postre de músico,* a chocolate-covered cluster of fresh almonds, hazelnuts and raisins; and *grageas,* almonds or hazelnuts drenched in dark chocolate, white chocolate or toffee.

RAMÓN ROCA is a large company set up in Gerona in 1928 by the Roca family. Roca chocolates are said to be a favourite of former US Secretary of State Henry Kissinger, and they certainly grace the tables of Spain's society élite, as well as finding their way on to first class intercontinental flights and the pillows of Spain's grandest hotels. Roca has always been imaginative in a showy type of way, producing masterpieces such as a 500g/1¼lb chocolate sculpture of the Statue of Liberty, and a hand-painted chocolate reproduction of the twelfth-century tapestry that hangs in Gerona cathedral. The company also

ABOVE: The Spanish love chocolate "a la taza" (in the cup).

produces a unique range of edible board games, particularly popular with the Japanese, which includes a draughts set in luxury dark and white chocolate. Their Victoria Bonbons (named after Ramón Roca's mother) — an elegant wafer of dark chocolate decorated with a perfectly positioned almond, a hazelnut, a walnut and four raisins — won first prize at the 1988 Chicago Fancy Food Fair.

RIGHT: The Valor range of chocolates.
LEFT: Chocolate croquettes from Roca.

VALOR in Villajoyosa, Alicante, was founded in 1881 by López Lloret, one of Spain's itinerant *chocolateros*. The fledgling enterprise has been handed down through three generations and is now one of Spain's largest and most technologically advanced chocolate companies with a gleaming stainless-steel fully computerized factory. Even though Valor has an enormous turnover and a vast range of products, the company prides itself on maintaining traditional quality, creativity and attention to detail.

Drinking chocolate is still widely enjoyed

RIGHT: Chunks of chocolate in tablet form, used in Spain for making thick, dark drinking chocolate.

in Spain, and Valor is the country's leading producer. It is sold both in powdered form and, more commonly, as a solid bar to be broken off as required and dissolved in foaming hot milk.

On the confectionery side, Valor's specialities are Chocolate Pearls – chocolate-covered almonds gathered from local almond groves; *doblones* – individually wrapped chocolate wafers; foil-wrapped hazelnut pralines; exquisite miniature four-piece gift boxes of chocolates; and luxury chocolate bars filled with toffee, cream caramel or *tiramisu*. Eye-catching and attractive packaging is a crucial part of the presentation, particularly as Valor's luxury chocolates are exported to speciality shops all over the world.

MEXICO

Chocolate as confectionery never really caught on in Mexico. The most important use of chocolate is still as a beverage, and as a flavouring in some of the special *moles* – rich, savoury sauces thickened with ground nuts and seeds. Chocolate is sold in rough, grainy tablets made with cacao, sugar, ground almonds and cinnamon – not so very different from the tablets made by the Spanish in the days of the conquistadors.

The most widely available brand outside Mexico is Ibarra, manufactured by CHOCOLATERA DE JALISCO in Guadalajara, and packaged in a striking red and yellow striped hexagonal box. The individually wrapped tablets are delicious whipped to a froth in hot milk and served with freshly baked *churros* (fried pastries).

RIGHT: Coarse, grainy tablets of Ibarra chocolate in traditional wrappers.
BELOW: The melted tablets make a delicious sauce for vanilla ice-cream.

They can be used in baking to give a unique spicy flavour to chocolate cake. The tablets can also be melted to make a wonderfully fudgey chocolate sauce that goes particularly well with good quality vanilla ice-cream.

GREAT BRITAIN

ABOVE: Ackermans chocolates, a favourite of the Royal family.

During the last few years British taste in chocolate has been undergoing a quiet revolution. Following the establishment of The Chocolate Society, a sort of sub-culture of chocolytes has emerged. Perhaps as a result of this new-found fervour, superior varieties of chocolate are increasingly finding their way into supermarkets, where they provide much-needed competition for the old-style sweet British milk chocolate.

ACKERMANS, a small family firm founded fifty years ago by German-born Werner Ackerman and his wife, is one of the major producers of handmade chocolates in Britain. Ackermans has a shop in north London, and also supplies leading supermarkets and specialist outlets in Britain, mainland Europe and the United States. Its chocolates are a favourite with Queen Elizabeth The Queen Mother, who awarded the firm her Royal Warrant in 1969. Ackermans offers a range of fresh cream truffles, chocolate-coated whole nuts, ginger wafers, hand-dipped crystallized fruits, and rose and violet fondant creams. It also produces a wonderful chocolate menagerie of hollow moulded hippos, crocodiles, bears and bunnies.

BENDICKS OF MAYFAIR, founded in the late 1920s by Colonel Benson and Mr Dickson, was granted a Royal Warrant by Elizabeth II in 1962. Bendicks are famous for their excellent peppermint chocolates – an essentially British taste not shared by other European countries. Best-loved by connoisseurs are Bendicks Bittermints, a powerful mint fondant disc drenched with smooth, dark unsweetened chocolate – a devastating combination. As well as the mint collection, Bendicks produces delicious truffles, chocolate-coated stem ginger, and the delightfully named Sporting & Military Chocolate.

CHARBONNEL ET WALKER, founded in 1825, is one of Britain's earliest producers of chocolates. With the encouragement of

BELOW: Bendicks are the premier supplier of superior mint chocolates.

BELOW: Exquisite chocolates from the Charbonnel et Walker range.

LEFT: Organic chocolate made with Maya beans.

Edward VII, the company began life as a partnership between Mrs Walker and Madame Charbonnel from the Maison Boissier chocolate house in Paris. Tempting items from the magnificent range include truffles flavoured with chartreuse, muscat or port and cranberry; chocolate-covered espresso beans; and cointreau-flavoured marzipan. The packaging is superb and caters for styles ranging from elegant navy-trimmed white boxes, nostalgic boxes with a faded pink floral pattern, and outrageously lavish, ruched red satin boxes.

GERARD RONAY is one of Britain's most highly respected private chocolatiers. A former psychiatric nurse, Ronay set up in 1989 having trained with the very best teachers – Linxe, Constant and Bernachon in France, Wittamer in Belgium and Charbonnel et Walker in Britain. His highly secretive recipes include geranium chocolate and superb hand-painted eggs.

GREEN AND BLACK'S, set up in the 1980s by Josephine Fairly, sells organic chocolate endorsed by The Soil Association. The company launched with its Organic Dark Chocolate, soon followed by its latest brain child, the "ethically correct" Maya Gold Organic Dark Chocolate, made with beans grown by the Kechi Maya in Belize. This product was the first in Britain to be awarded the Fairtrade mark which guarantees that small farmers are not exploited. Maya Gold contains 70 per cent cacao solids, but no cacao butter, and is described on the wrapper as having "the authentic Maya taste of rain forest spices and

BELOW: Rococo's grand cru single bean bars with distinctive wrappers.

ABOVE: A tempting and imaginative range from The Chocolate Society.

orange". Even though oranges were unknown to the Maya in pre-Conquest days, the chocolate still tastes pretty good.

ROCOCO, in London's King's Road, is an Aladdin's cave of a shop founded in 1983 by chocolate enthusiast Chantal Coady. Using cacao from the world's finest plantations, Rococo specialize in *grand cru* single bean bars; artisan bars with exotic flavourings such as pink pepper and juniper, lavender, petitgrain and cardamom; stunning chocolate dragées – try the dark green *Olives de Nyons;* and handmade boxed chocolates moulded into the most beautiful shapes.

SARA JAYNE, a London-based private chocolate-maker, is also public relations manager of the Académie Culinaire de France. She learnt her chocolate-making skills first hand from leading experts, including the Roux brothers. Blackberry and calvados, ginger and spice, and champagne are among the tempting flavourings used in her celebrated handmade truffles.

TERRYS OF YORK, founded in 1797, is perhaps alone among the mass-producers in manufacturing plain chocolate with a reasonable flavour. Their famous chocolate orange has been tucked in the toe of British children's Christmas stockings for generations, while their individually wrapped miniature Neapolitans have always been a welcome gift.

THE CHOCOLATE SOCIETY was formed in 1990 to promote the consumption of the finest chocolate. The society manufactures a range of products under its own label, as well as selling quality brands made by other companies. Its own range includes the most delicious chocolate-dipped candied citrus fruits; imaginative moulded items such as pigs, egg-filled nests, fish, hens and hearts; fresh handmade truffles with luscious flavourings such as raspberry, whisky or champagne; and elegant tins of drinking-chocolate flakes, cocoa powder and cooking chocolate.

THE UNITED STATES OF AMERICA

Chocolate consumers in the United States share the British liking for sweet milk chocolate, and the American chocolate industry is therefore dominated by a small number of very large mass-producers who satisfy this national need. However, in the same way that British consumers have become aware of and learned to appreciate quality handmade plain chocolate, American taste has been changing too. A number of small but sophisticated chocolate-makers have appeared on the scene and are taking advantage of the increasing popularity of European-style chocolate.

ABOVE: Glossy sugar-coated dragées from Dilettante.

DILETTANTE, in Seattle, was established in 1976 by Dana Davenport, a third-generation chocolatier and descendant of Hungarian master chocolatier Julius Franzen. Franzen emigrated to the USA in 1910, after studying in Paris, and won prestigious appointments in Vienna as Master Pâtissier to Emperor Franz Joseph, and later in St Petersburg as Master Chocolatier to Czar Nicholas II. Franzen passed on his skills to his brother-in-law Earl Remington Davenport, whose grandson Dana carries on the business today. Dilettante's signature product is its Aristocrat range of chocolate truffles, flavoured with ginger, raspberries, hazelnuts, pecans or coffee. Dilettante also makes intensely rich buttercream fondant, beautiful chocolate dragées with various coatings, and slim bars of good quality milk or dark chocolate.

ABOVE AND RIGHT: Ghirardelli, new and old.

FRAN'S, set up in Seattle by ex-accountant Fran Bigelow, is at the forefront of America's new generation of chocolatiers. She trained in cookery under

Josephine Araldo, a 1921 graduate of the Cordon Bleu school in Paris, and later enrolled at the California Culinary Academy, where desserts became her passion. Bigelow opened a tiny dessert shop in 1982, supplying local restaurants with speciality cakes. Her reputation went from strength to strength, and, soon after, she started making the European-style chocolates on which her business is now founded. An award-winning speciality are Fran's baton-shaped Fixations — individual sticks of Belgian chocolate with soft, creamy centres, flavoured with espresso, peanut butter, orange or mint. Her range also includes rich dark truffles, hand-dipped fruit and nuts covered in smooth dark Belgian chocolate, GoldBars studded with macadamia nuts, and the smaller GoldBites with almonds, as well as chocolate and caramel sauces, and various seasonal items.

GHIRARDELLI, founded in 1856 in San Francisco and one of

ABOVE: Irresistible luxury from Fran's.

RIGHT: Joseph Schmidt's stunning truffles.

America's pioneering chocolate-makers, produces quality eating chocolate, chocolate products for use in baking, and powdered drinking chocolate. Ghirardelli's Sweet Ground Chocolate with Cocoa has been a signature product for over a century. Although a mass producer, Ghirardelli uses methods based on European traditions, producing bittersweet eating chocolate as well as the popular sweet milk varieties. Ghirardelli still grinds and roasts its own cacao beans shipped from quality plantations in Central and South America, and West Africa. Its range includes milk, white and plain chocolate squares and attractively wrapped bars with tempting flavours such as raspberry, white mocha and biscotti, and double chocolate mocha.

JOSEPH SCHMIDT CONFECTIONS was opened in San Francisco in 1983 by master chocolatier Joseph Schmidt and partner Audrey Ryan. Born in 1939 and raised in what was formerly known as Palestine, Schmidt looks to his Austrian roots for his skills. He was trained as a baker, but his supremely imaginative and sometimes outrageous creations show no evidence of this conventional background. Unusual in the chocolate world for his bold use of colour, and the large size of the individual chocolates, Schmidt's truffles gleam with perfect hand-painted spots of bright red or green, and his Slicks, thin chocolate discs, are beautifully painted in various colours. Special commissions include amazingly opulent sculpted creations for visiting dignitaries from abroad – including a giant panda for Prince Philip and a

RIGHT: Elegance from Richard Donnelly.

white dove for Nelson Mandela. Schmidt's chocolates are available from department stores in the United States and Harrods in London.

RICHARD DONNELLY, in Santa Cruz, California, is another of America's new breed of young, inspired artisan chocolate-makers.

Donnelly trained with several renowned chocolatiers both in Europe and the United States before setting up on his own in 1988. Donnelly uses French couverture chocolate to which he adds flavourings and fillings geared to the American market – coffee buttercream, and roasted salted macadamia nuts, for instance. His speciality is very slim, smooth chocolate bars which, in terms of quality, are among the very best chocolate in the world. The bars are beautifully wrapped in handmade Japanese papers.

MOONSTRUCK CHOCOLATIER in Portland, Oregon, is a young company set up by an impressive consortium of live-wire marketing experts. With more then a hundred outlets in the United States and a thriving mail order business they look set to make their name in the world of chocolate.

Moonstruck's chocolates are inspired creations from master chocolatier Robert Hammond, who served his apprenticeship in America and France, and who is now thought to be one of the leading experts in modern chocolate-making. Moonstruck's signature product is a moon-shaped, metallic blue box containing a stunning selection of beautifully designed chocolates. Flavourings include wine, brandy, coffee, *sake* and various fruits, often using award-winning local products. Favourites are wild huckleberry truffles made with white chocolate ganache and Clear Creek apple brandy truffles. There is also an impressive *gianduja* almond praline tower of crisp buttery toffee and toasted almonds.

PHYSIOLOGY AND PSYCHOLOGY

CHOCOLATE'S THERAPEUTIC POWERS

The therapeutic properties of chocolate were much written about in the seventeenth and eighteenth centuries. The Aztec beliefs in the power of chocolate travelled with it, and great claims were made by manufacturers and converts alike for its powers as an antidote to exhaustion and weakness. Soldiers, scholars and clerics used it to keep them going during prolonged periods of physical, intellectual or spiritual endurance.

We now know that it is the fat and carbohydrate in chocolate which provide fuel for the body, and the fat content means that chocolate is digested slowly, thus maintaining a feeling of fullness and satiety. Even the iron content, which helps transport oxygen to the brain, may result in greater mental alertness, although this has yet to be proven.

(PER 100G)	PLAIN CHOCOLATE	MILK CHOCOLATE	WHITE CHOCOLATE
Protein (g)	4.7	8.4	8.0
Fat (g)	29.2	30.3	30.9
Calories	525	529	529
Carbohydrate (g)	64.8	59.4	58.3
Calcium (mg)	38	220	270
Magnesium (mg)	100	55	26
Iron (mg)	2.4	1.6	0.2
Zinc (mg)	0.2	0.2	0.9
Carotene (vitamin A) (mcg)	40	40	75
Vitamin E (mg)	0.85	0.74	1.14
Thiamin (vitamin B1) (mg)	0.07	0.10	0.08
Riboflavin (vitamin B2) (mg)	0.08	0.23	0.49
Niacin (vitamin B3) (mg)	0.4	0.2	0.2
Vitamin B6 (mg)	0.07	0.07	0.07
Vitamin B12 (mcg)	—	trace	trace
Folate (mcg)	10	10	10
Vitamin C	0	0	0

Source: McCance and Widdowson's The Composition of Foods, fifth edition.

NUTRITIONAL ANALYSIS

Although the relevance of nutritional analysis is questionable if the level of cacao solids or brand of chocolate used is not known, we can see from the comparative table above that plain chocolate, considered by the chocolate fraternity as infinitely superior, does not fare as well as might be expected.

Containing no milk, plain chocolate provides roughly half the protein of white and milk chocolate, and much less calcium. Protein is vital for the growth, repair and maintenance of the body; calcium is essential for muscle contraction, including the muscles which make the heart beat, and for healthy nerve function, enzyme activity and clotting of blood.

LEFT: Early publicity material depicted cocoa as wholesome.
RIGHT: Chocolate fortified the army in the First World War.

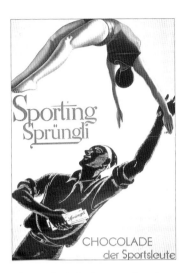

ABOVE: Carbohydrate in chocolate provides fuel for vigorous activity.

Plain chocolate contains slightly less fat, something we are advised to cut down on, and comes out on top in terms of carbohydrate, magnesium (an essential constituent of our body cells and involved with releasing energy from the food we eat), iron (essential for the production of red blood cells, and for transporting oxygen around the body) and niacin (also involved in energy release from food). Plain chocolate also contains slightly fewer calories. White chocolate, sometimes dismissed by chocolate experts, contains more calcium, zinc, carotene and riboflavin (vitamin B2) than plain chocolate.

A NATURAL STIMULANT

As well as the more well-known nutrients, chocolate contains certain alkaloids – organic substances found in plants – which have a potent effect on the body. The most important is theobromine, which stimulates the kidneys as a mild diuretic. Chocolate is also a stimulant of the central nervous system, with an effect similar to caffeine, which is also present in chocolate. Theobromine makes up about 2 per cent of the cacao bean and about 200 mg finds its way into an average-sized bar. The caffeine content is much smaller – about 25 mg per bar, roughly one quarter the amount found in a fresh cup of coffee.

BELOW RIGHT: Many manufacturers depicted chocolate as providing growing children with plenty of energy for healthy activity.

— HOMEOPATHIC "PROVING" OF CHOCOLATE —

Experimental "provings" of chocolate by homeopaths clearly indicate its stimulating effect. One experiment conducted with a decoction of roasted ground cacao beans in boiling water produced "an excitement of the nervous system similar to that caused by a strong infusion of black coffee" and "an excited state of the circulation, shown by an accelerated pulse". Interestingly, when the same decoction was made with unroasted beans neither effect was noticeable, leading the provers to conclude that the physiological changes were caused by aromatic substances released during roasting.

— MYTHS AND PREJUDICES —

Claims that chocolate is bad for you are almost certainly based on the excess sugar and added vegetable fat in poor grade, mass-produced chocolate. Quality chocolate contains pure cacao butter with no added fat, as well as a high percentage of cacao solids and correspondingly less sugar – in some cases hardly any. Specific claims that chocolate causes migraine, obesity, acne, tooth decay and allergies have also been refuted by several medical experts:

MIGRAINE Cheese and chocolate have been cited as the cause of migraine, which can be set off by large doses of tyramine. Chocolate, however, contains only a very small quantity of tyramine, far less than cheese.

OBESITY Good quality plain chocolate is unlikely to be the cause of obesity because it contains far less sugar than junk chocolate and, because it is more expensive, is less likely to be eaten to excess.

ACNE American surveys show no correlation between chocolate consumption and acne in teenagers. Likely culprits are hormonal imbalances and a lack of fresh fruit and vegetables in the diet.

TOOTH DECAY Chocolate melts in the mouth and is therefore in contact with the teeth for a relatively short time. While the sugar content will contribute to tooth decay, the risk is far less than that associated with sticky sweets or toffee, which remain in the mouth for longer.

ALLERGY Less than 2 per cent of the population have a genuine food allergy, and an allergy to chocolate is extremely rare. It is more likely to be the nuts and milk in chocolate that are the cause, so check the ingredients.

CHOCOLATE AND THE MIND

The question of whether or not chocolate is an addictive substance always raises spirited discussion. Some social historians have even reported tales of chocolate addiction and associated crimes committed in order to satisfy an ever-increasing need. And as recently as 1991, the French dietary expert Michel Montignac advised in his book *Dine Out and Lose Weight:* "Be sure to limit yourself, since chocolate is of an addictive nature. To control your 'chocoholism', drink a tall glass of water."

LEFT: A deeply indulgent chocolate experience.

Linda Henly, a contemporary American writer, positively recommends that addictive personalities should use chocolate to satisfy their needs, stating that its advantages vastly outweigh those of other substances: "Chocolate doesn't make you stupid and clumsy. It doesn't render you incapable of operating heavy machinery… You don't have to smuggle chocolate across the border…Possession, even possession with intent to sell, is perfectly legal."

Some medical experts believe that the theobromine and caffeine in chocolate are the cause of its so-called addictive properties, but it may well be the presence of another substance called phenylethylamine. This is one of a group of chemicals known as endorphins, which have an effect similar to amphetamine, to which phenylethylamine is related. When released into the bloodstream, endorphins lift the mood, creating positive energy and feelings ranging from happiness to euphoria, as experienced in the runner's "high" or the aerobic exerciser's "burn". Phenylethylamine is also naturally present in the human body. Levels in the brain have even been found to increase when we experience the state we refer to as "falling in love", which is no doubt why we experience that heady feeling when we eat good chocolate.

CRAVING AND ADDICTION

Chocolate lovers would do well to be aware of the wealth of difference there is between craving and addiction. Craving is an unmet desire for a pleasurable substance, whether it be chocolate, hot buttered toast, or a cup of coffee. The craving is usually brought on by stress, and the desired substance usually diffuses the stress more effectively than any other means, and may actually, as a result, enhance a person's performance by increasing concentration and reducing fatigue.

Addiction, on the other hand, is defined as the habitual use of a substance, such as alcohol or drugs, which becomes less and less effective at satisfying the need and results in unpleasant withdrawal symptoms should any attempt be made to give up the substance in question.

Chocolate hardly comes into the addictive category, although it has been said that the glucose in chocolate triggers a release in the production of endorphins – the body's natural opiates – which in turn can lead to a cycle of craving.

LEFT: A silver platter of gorgeous, high quality, hand-made chocolates is every chocolate lover's fantasy.

BELOW: An advertisement showing two French ladies sharing a bottle of chocolate as if it were wine. The initial effect can be very similar.

RIGHT: *Dark, rich and irresistible, a slice of moist chocolate cake is both pleasure and temptation.*

BELOW: *French courtesan and famous chocolyte, Madame Du Barry, was well aware of the stimulating effect chocolate had on her lovers.*

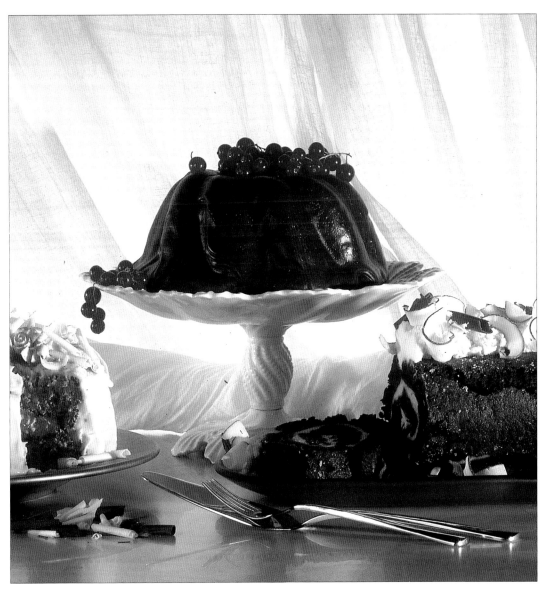

WOMEN'S CRAVING AND CHOCOLATE

Women are the greatest consumers of chocolate, and several studies have sought to explain why. Although some women may enjoy chocolate as a guilt-free treat or as an energy-boost, others seem almost obsessed by it. While researching her 1995 book *Why Women Need Chocolate*, Debra Waterhouse conducted a survey which revealed that of the women surveyed:

- 97 per cent reported cravings, 68 per cent of which are for chocolate
- 50 per cent would choose chocolate in preference to sex
- 22 per cent were more likely than men to choose chocolate as a mood elevator

Psychiatrists have suggested that the mechanism that regulates body levels of phenylethylamine may be faulty in some women. This may explain a tendency to binge on chocolate after an emotional upset – it is an instinctive form of self-medication to treat the imbalance of mood-controlling chemicals.

Waterhouse states that the foods we crave are defined by a multitude of factors that may include cultural influences, emotional attachments, taste and habit as well as biological, chemical and physiological factors. In the case of chocolate, the "prozac of plants", Waterhouse adds to its mood-changing components a substance called seratonin, known for its calming properties.

It must be said, however, that although statistically it may be the case that more women buy chocolate than men, it is also true that for both sexes, and for people of all ages, chocolate can be many things. There are probably many women who could instantly name a man whose chocolate consumption is more regular and compulsive than hers, and it is perhaps one of the many cultural myths that women are more addicted to it than men. What we can say is that the seduction of chocolate, and its comforting allure, is as strong in the present as it was for the Maya warrior princes and princesses of the fourth century.

CHOCOLATE AND LOVE

Chocolate has long been associated with passion and its reputation as an aphrodisiac can be traced back to the days of the Aztecs and the Spanish conquistadors. Conclusions were obviously drawn from the Emperor Montezuma's liking for copious flagons of chocolate before retiring to his harem. However, as observer Bernal Díaz del Castillo was careful to point out in his memoirs: "It [chocolate] was said to have aphrodisiac properties, but we did not pay any attention to this detail."

In *The True History of Chocolate* authors Sophie and Michael Coe state that the idea that Montezuma needed sexual stimulants was a Spanish obsession for which there was no factual basis. The conquistadors apparently suffered from constipation and "searched for native Mexican laxatives as avidly as they did for aphrodisiacs". However, once the rumour that chocolate was an aphrodisiac had taken root, there was no stopping it. When chocolate eventually appeared in Europe, eighteenth-century society took to it with suspicious enthusiasm.

Historical sources abound with tales of chocolate being used as an aphrodisiac. Casanova thought that hot chocolate was "the elixir of love", and drank it instead of champagne! It may well be that the unshakeable belief of the Spanish had something to do with chocolate being an ingredient in that notorious aphrodisiac "Spanish Fly". In the following tale, the Marquis de Sade uses both chocolate and Spanish fly to amuse his guests at a ball: "Into the dessert he slipped chocolate pastilles so good that a number of people devoured them … but he had mixed in some Spanish fly … those who ate the pastilles began to burn with unchaste ardor … Even the most respectable of women were unable to resist the uterine rage that stirred within them. And so it was that M. de Sade enjoyed the favors of his sister-in-law."

RIGHT: An early Cadbury chocolate tin uses sensual imagery.

THE GREAT INFLAMER

Brandon Head, in *The Food of the Gods,* reported that even after chocolate had become widely accepted as a nourishing beverage, it was still regarded by some "as a violent inflamer of passions, which should be prohibited to the monks". In 1905 a journalist writing in the British Spectator magazine issued dire warnings: 'I shall also advise my fair readers to be in a particular manner careful how they meddle with romances, chocolates, novels, and the like inflamers, which I look upon as very dangerous to be made use of…"

SENSUAL ASSOCIATIONS

Although contemporary scientific research suggests that chocolate does not contain substances of a directly aphrodisiac nature, modern advertising clearly links chocolate with sensuality and sexuality. With the exception of chunky "macho" chocolate products, or situations in which the product is being used as a healthy, energy-boosting snack, chocolate is invariably depicted as a "naughty" indulgence, appearing in scenes heavy with sexual innuendo.

Advertising also demonstrates a definite gender bias by specifically targeting women as the primary users. Most advertisements show chocolate being enjoyed by beautiful

LEFT AND RIGHT: The images may not be as explicit as today, but advertising has always used chocolate's link with sensuality to sell its products.

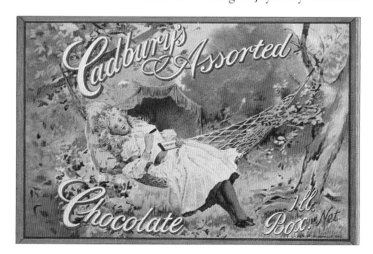

advertising made much of the wholesomeness of chocolate with posters of healthy, lively children enjoying cups of chocolate in the fresh air. The first chocolate boxes showed sentimental images of pretty young girls, flowers and kittens. Chocolate plays a large part in childhood the world over. Christmas treats, Easter eggs, birthday presents, party gifts, rewards or bribes from parents coaxing their offspring to behave well. Encouraged as most of us are to be passionate about chocolate from an early age, it is no wonder we carry that ardour with us through childhood and beyond.

ABOVE: A poster illustrating the link between lovers and chocolate.

RIGHT: The famous Rowntree advertisement.

BELOW: A loving mother offers chocolate to her daughter.

women, or gifts of chocolate being offered to them by a man.

The association between women, sensuality and chocolate was reinforced by the cinema, too. A common image in the 1930s was the glamorous *femme fatale*, usually blonde and usually draped on satin sheets, languorously working her way through a lavish box of chocolates.

This association between chocolate and women perpetuated the association between chocolate and romantic love, as shown on Perugina's classic Baci box. *Baci* means "kisses" in Italian, and since the chocolates first appeared in 1922 they have been exchanged as gifts between lovers who look for the romantic message hidden beneath the foil wrapper of each chocolate.

CHOCOLATE AND CHILDHOOD

This association with love and nurture, but not necessarily passion, was also exploited by manufacturers. Chocolate cake mix packets carry homely scenes of mother in the kitchen; the earliest cocoa tins portrayed nursemaids or even parents serving nourishing mugs of chocolate to young children, and

THE PLEASURE OF CHOCOLATE

Research carried out by ARISE (Associates for Research Into the Science of Enjoyment) suggests that pleasure, far from being an emotion of indeterminate nature, is a distinct neuro-chemical process with its own pathway through the nervous system. Laboratory tests have shown that when we are experiencing pleasure, the body's defence system is more effective; and when we are unhappy, depressed or stressed, the system becomes less efficient, leaving us less resistant to infection.

So it seems that pleasure is good for us even if it means we indulge in "forbidden fruits" such as chocolate. The secret, it would seem, is to indulge in our "naughty" craving without feeling guilty or anxious. That said, ARISE make it clear that they are not advocating orgies of over-indulgence; the secret is to eat better chocolate, not more chocolate.

SENSORY PLEASURE

One of the reasons we love chocolate so much is the pure unmatched physical pleasure we get not just from eating it, but also from unwrapping it, smelling it, looking at it and feeling it. When we slip the wrapper off a slim bar of dark chocolate or open up the softly padded papers of a luxury box, our sense of anticipation is already at work. The pure chocolatey smell is like perfume and the chocolate looks so smooth and glossy we want to stroke it. Breaking off a piece, it snaps cleanly with a pleasing crack. When it finally passes the lips, chocolate melts instantly in the mouth – an exquisitely pleasurable sensation. Then the flavours come flooding through – overwhelming our taste buds with over five hundred of them, two-and-a-half times more than any other food. With such a wealth of sensory pleasure in store, no wonder chocolate should be eaten slowly.

Whether or not we choose to share our pleasure with others by attempting to describe the complex flavours is another matter. The current passion for chocolate indicates that perhaps a tasting language will evolve along the same lines as that used for wine and, more recently, olive oil. At the moment, fellow chocolate lovers get by without a specialized vocabulary – they just know when it is good and a roll of the eyes or a deep sigh is enough to communicate this.

Elaine Sherman, a twentieth-century American writer, more than adequately sums up: "Chocolate is heavenly, mellow, sensual, deep, dark, sumptuous, gratifying, potent, dense, creamy,

BELOW: Chocolate provides unmatched sensory pleasure – a delight to look at, a pleasure to touch, wonderful to smell and pleasurable to eat.

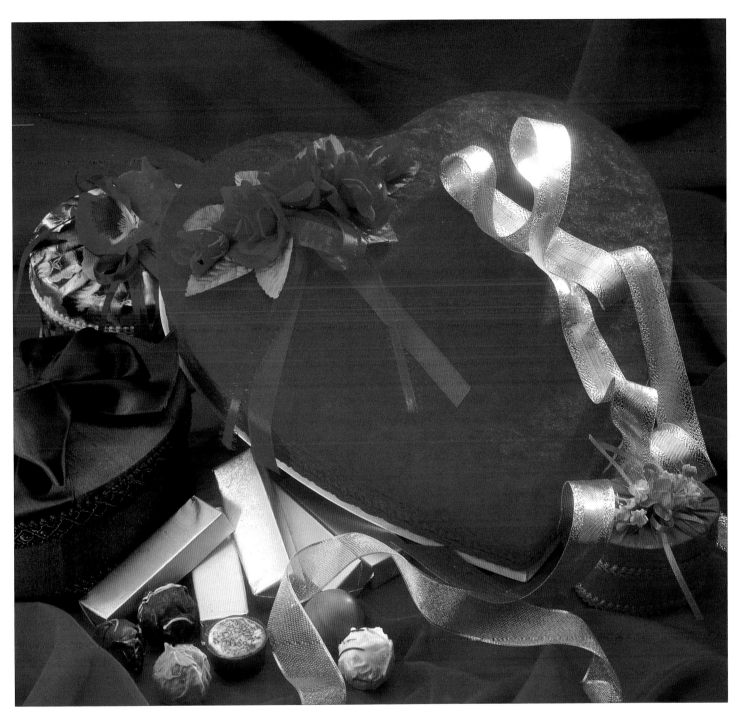

ABOVE: Chocolate has been used as a gift since the days of the Aztecs. It speaks a thousand words and feelings.

seductive, suggestive, rich, excessive, silky, smooth, luxurious, celestial. Chocolate is downfall, happiness, pleasure, love, ecstasy, fantasy … chocolate makes us wicked, guilty, sinful, healthy, chic, happy."

A CULTURAL AND SOCIAL LUBRICANT

Chocolate has always been used as a gift. As Michel Richart, an inspired chocolate-maker in Lyon, rightly states, when we share good quality chocolate it weaves links between people on many, many levels. Chocolate also creates valuable cultural, social and even spiritual awareness.

A small box of luxury chocolates says a thousand "thank-you's" to a hostess, a mother or a lover. Chocolate also says "good luck", "congratulations", "bon voyage" and "sorry". Queen Victoria symbolically sent 5,000 lbs/2,268 kg chocolate to her loyal troops at Christmas. Sales of chocolate rocket on Mother's Day and Valentine's Day. We use it in one form or another to celebrate Easter, Christmas and weddings.

There is hardly a country in the western world that does not have chocolate as part of its culinary culture, whether it be a moist chocolate brownie from America, a chocolate-covered pancake from Hungary, a velvety square of Swiss milk fondant chocolate, or a foaming cup of thick Spanish drinking chocolate. It is these chocolate "experiences" that unite chocolate lovers throughout the world in celebration of the food of the gods.

CHOCOLATE SUPPLIERS AROUND THE WORLD

AUSTRALIA
Chocolatier Australia
224 Waterdale Road, Ivanhoe,
Victoria 3079 Tel: (3) 94 99 70 22

The Chocolate Box
761 Burke Road, Camberwell,
Victoria 3124 Tel: (3) 98 13 13 77

Darren Taylor's Handmade Chocolates
Seet Art, 96 Oxford Street, Paddington,
New South Wales 2021
Tel: (2) 93 61 66 17

Sweet William Chocolates
4 William Street, Paddington, New
South Wales 2021 Tel: (2) 93 31 54 68

Simon Johnson
181 Harris Street, Pyrmont, New South
Wales 2009 Tel: (2) 95 52 25 22

Haigh's Chocolates
Beehive Corner, 2 Rundle Mall,
Adelaide, South Australia
Tel: (8) 23 12 844

AUSTRIA
Altmann & Kühne
Graben 30, 1010 Wien
Tel: (1) 53 30 927

Demels
14 Kohlmarkt, 1010 Wien
Tel: (1) 53 51 717

Hotel Imperial
Kärtner Ring 16, A-1051 Wien
Tel: (1) 50 11 03 13
Fax: (1) 50 10 355

Mirabell Salzburger Confiserie
Hauptstrasse 14-16, A-5082 Grödig
Tel: (62) 46 20 110

BELGIUM
Charlemagne
Place Jacques Brel 8, 4040 Herstal
Tel: (41) 64 66 44

Godiva
Wapenstilstandstraat 5, 1081 Brussels
Tel: (2) 42 21 711

Kim's Chocolates
Nieuwlandlaan 12, Industriezone B-615,
B-3200 Aarschot
Tel: (16) 55 15 80

Neuhaus
Postbox 2, B - 1602 Vlenzenbeek
Tel: (2) 56 82 211

Pierre Colas
2 Rue Campagne, 4577 Modave
Tel: (2) 64 80 893

Wittamer
12 Place du Grand Sablon, Grote Zavel
12, 1000 Brussels Tel: (2) 51 28 451

FRANCE
Bonnat
8 Cours Senozan, 38500 Voiron
Tel: (76) 05 28 09

Christian Constant
26 Rue du Bac, 75007 Paris
Tel: (47) 03 30 00

Cluizel
La Fontaine au Chocolat
101 & 210 Rue Saint Honoré,
75001 Paris Tel: (1) 42 44 11 66

Fauchon
26-30 Place de la Madeleine,
75008 Paris Tel: (1) 47 42 60 11

Lalonde
59 Rue St Dizier, 54400 Nancy
Tel: 83 53 31 57

La Maison du Chocolat
225 Rue Faubourg St Honoré,
75008 Paris Tel: (1) 42 27 39 44

Le Roux
18 Rue du Port-Maria, 56170 Quiberon
Tel: 97 50 06 83

Richart Design et Chocolat
258 Bd. Saint-Germain, 75007 Paris
Tel: (1) 45 55 66 00

Chocolaterie Valrhona
BP 40, 26600 Tain L'Hermitage
Tel: 75 07 90 90

Weiss
18 Avenue Denfert-Rochereau,
42000 St Etienne
Tel: 77 49 41 41

GERMANY
Confiserie Heinemann
Krefelder Strasse 645
41066 München-Gladbach
Tel: (2161) 6930

Dreimeister
Weststrasse 47 - 49, Werl,
Westönnen Tel: 29 22 8 20 45

Feodora
Vertriebszentrale Bremen,
Postfach 105803, D28058 Bremen
Tel: (421) 59 90 61

Bremer Chocolade-Fabrik Hachez
Westerstrasse 32, D-28199 Bremen
Tel: (421) 59 50 64 62

Leysieffer
Benzstrasse 9, 49076 Osnabrück
Tel: (541) 91 420

Stollwerck
Stollwerckstrasse 27-31, 51149 Köln
Tel: (22) 03 430

Van Houten
Am Stamgleis, 22844 Norderstedt
Tel: (5) 26 020

GREAT BRITAIN
Ackermans
9 Goldhurst Terrace, Finchley Road,
London, NW6 3HX
Tel: (0171) 624 2742

Charbonnel et Walker
1 The Royal Arcade, 28 Old Bond
Street, London, W1X 4BT
Tel: (0171) 491 0939

Gerard Ronay
3 Warple Way, London, W3 0RF
Tel: (0181) 730 818

Godiva
247 Regent Street, London, W1
Tel: (0171) 409 0963

Grania & Sarnia
6 Sterne Street, London, W12 8AD
Tel: (0181) 749 8274

Green & Black
Whole Earth Food, 269 Portobello
Road, London, W1 1LR
Tel: (0171) 229 7545

JB Confectionery
Unit 3, The Palmerston Centre,
Oxford Road, Harrow, Middlesex,
HA3 7RG Tel: (0181) 863 0011

Mortimer & Bennett
33 Turnham Green Terrace, London,
W4 1RG Tel: (0181) 995 4145

Rococo Chocolates
321 Kings Road, London, SW3 5EP
Tel: (0171) 352 5857
Fax: (0171) 352 7360

Sara Jayne
517 Old York Road, London, SW18 1TF
Tel: (0181) 874 8500

The Chocolate Society
Clay Pit Lane, Roecliffe, Near
Boroughbridge, N. Yorks, YO5 9LS
Tel: (01423) 322 230

The Cool Chile Company
P.O. Box 5702, London, W11 2GS
Tel: (0171) 229 9360

Town & Country Chocolates
52 Oxford Road, Denham, Uxbridge,
Middlesex, UB9 4DH
Tel: (01895) 256 166

ITALY
Caffarel/Peyrano
Via Gianevello 41 - 10062 Luserna,
S. Giovanni (TO), Piedmont
Tel: (121) 90 10 86

Maglio Arte Dolciaria
73024 Maglio, La Via Gioacchino
Toma 4 Tel: (836) 25 723

Majani
Via Lunga 19/C, Crespellano (BO)
Tel: 51 96 91 57

Perugina
Nestlé Italiana
Via Pievaiola, San Sisto, PGIT
Tel: (75) 52 761

MEXICO
Chocolatera de Jalisco
Av Narianotero 1420, Apartado Postal
33121, 44510 Guadalajara, Halisco

SPAIN
Blanxart
Tambor del Bruc, 13-08970 Sant Joan
Despi, Barcelona Tel: (3) 373 3761

Ludomar
Ciudad de la Asunción 58, 08030
Barcelona Tel: (72) 203 662

Ramón Roca
Mercaders, 6 17004, Gerona
Tel: (72) 203 662

Chocolates Valor
Pianista Gonzalo Soriano, 13 Villajoyosa
Tel: (6) 589 050

SWITZERLAND
Lindt & Sprüngli
Seestrasse 204, CH-8802 Kilchberg
Tel: (1) 71 62 233

Sprüngli
Bahnhofstrasse 21, 8022 Zurich
Tel: (1) 21 15 777

THE NETHERLANDS
Bensdorp
Heerenstraat 51, Postbus 4, 1400 AA
Bussum Tel: (35) 69 74 911

Gerkens Cacao
Veerdijk 82, Postbus 82, 1530 AB
Wormer Tel: (35) 69 74 911

Cacao De Zaan
Stationsstraat 76, Postbus 2, 1540 AA
Koog aan de Zaan
Tel: (75) 62 83 601

Droste
PO Box 5, 8170AA Vaassen
Tel: (578) 57 82 00

USA
Dilettante Chocolates
416 Broadway, Seattle, WA 98102
Tel: (206) 328 1530

Fran's
2805 East Madison, Seattle, Washington,
WA 98122-4020
Tel: (206) 322 0233

Ghirardelli
900 North Point Street, San Francisco,
CA 94109 Tel: (415) 474 1414

Joseph Schmidt Confections
3489 16th Street, San Francisco,
CA 9411 Tel: (415) 861 8682

Richard Donnelly Fine Chocolates
1509 Mission Street, Santa Cruz,
CA 95060 Tel: (408) 458 4214

Moonstruck Chocolatier
6663 SW BVTN Hillsdale Highway,
STE194, Portland, Oregon, OR9 7225
Tel: (503) 283 8843

ACKNOWLEDGEMENTS
Thanks to the following companies for
supplying chocolates for photography:

Ackermans, Alfred Ritter, Bendicks
(Mayfair) Ltd, Charbonnel et Walker,
The Cool Chile Company, The
Chocolate Society, Richard Donnelly,
Feodora Chocolate, Ghirardelli
Chocolate Company, Grania & Sarni,
Green and Black, The Jenks Group, JB
Confectionery, Leonidas, Lessiters,
Nestlé Rowntree Ltd, Parsons Trading
Ltd, Perugina, Richart Design et
Chocolat, Rococo, Ryne Quality
Confectionery, Joseph Schmidt, Town &
Country Chocolates, Trustin.

Thanks also to Stefano Raimondi of the
Italian Trade Centre, Patrizia De Vito of
the Associazione Industrie Dolciarie in
Rome, Elaine Ashton of Grania and
Sarnia, Dan Mortimer of Mortimer and
Bennet, David Lyle of Town and Country
Chocolates and John Bacon of JB
Confectionery.
    Christine McFadden is particularly
indebted to the late Sophie Coe, and her
husband Michael Coe, for their book *The
True History of Chocolate*, and to Chantal
Coady for the information in *The
Chocolate Companion*.

INDEX

PICTURE ACKNOWLEDGEMENTS

Thanks to the following picture libraries for supplying additional images in the book.
AKG, London: pp7(br) *Columbus discovers the New World,* Bernhard Rode; 8(br) *First landing on Guanaja,* wood engraving; 19(b) *Goethe in the Countryside,* Johann Tischbein; 22(b) *Healing plants, cacao,* from FE Bilz; 59(tr) Poster for chocolate, *Mother's Cocoa in Danger.*

Bridgeman Art Library: pp16(r) *The chocolate girl,* Jean-Etienne Liotard, Dresden Gemäldegalerie; 17 *Still life,* Philippe Rousseau, Musée des Beaux Arts, Reims, Peter Willi; 18(t) *Cardinal Mazarin,* French School, Musée Condé, Chantilly; 18(bl) *Tapestry of Louis XIV's marriage,* Gobelins, Mobilier National, Paris; 20(br) *A cup of chocolate,* Sir John Lavery, Whitford and Hughes, London; 21(r) American poster for chocolate; 30(b) *Cocoa plantation in the Isle of Grenada,* O'Shea Gallery, London; 58(bl) *Cacao Van Houten,* Privet Livemont, Victoria and Albert, London; 58(br) Box of Cadbury's assorted chocolates, c1913.
    Mansell Collection: p23(b).
    Public Records Office : pp9(t); 25(t); 26(t); 28(br); 55(br).
    Visual Arts Library: pp6(l); 7(l);

8(bl) *Montezuma offering chocolate to Hernan Cortés,* PG Miguel, Artephot/Oronoz; 13(t) *Mexican making chocolate,* Codex Tuleda, Artephot/Oronoz; 18(r) *A horseman and a lady drinking chocolate,* Bonnart, Vision; 23(l) *Still Life: Chocolate set,* Luis Melendez, Museo del Prado, Madrid, Artephot/Oronoz; 24(b) *The morning cocoa,* Longhi; 25(tr) *The breakfast,* François Boucher, Musée du Louvre, Artephot/Oronoz; 25(tl) *Physiologie du Goût ou Méditations de Gastronomie Transcendante,* E Baneste; 27(br) *Advertisement, Chocolat Menier,* F Bouisset, Artephot/Perrin; 14(tl) *Cacao Van Houten,* Artephot/Perrin; 14(tr) Poster for Chocolate, H Gerbault; 46(tl) Poster for French Chocolate and Tea Company, Steilen, Artephot/Perrin; 47(l) Chocolat Capentier poster; 56(br) Chocolat Mondia, Artephot/Vision; 57(l) *Portrait of Madame Du Barry,* Greuze, Artephot/Varga; 59(br) *Chocolat Masson,* Grasset, Artephot/Perrin.
    Other pictures supplied courtesy of Bendick's (Mayfair) Ltd: 14(bl), Cadburys Ltd: 26(bl); 40(b); 41(bl); 58(tr). Fran's: 60. Godiva: 35(bl) 56(t). Nestlé Rowntree Ltd: 1; 25(b); 32(br) 34(tr&l), Rococo: 15(bl).

SELECTED BIBLIOGRAPHY

NATHALIE BAILLEUX, HERVÉ BIZEUL, JOHN FELTWELL, RÉGINE KOPP, CORBY KUMMER, PIERRE LABANNE, CRISTINA PAULY, ODILE PERRARD, MARIAROSA SCHIAFFINO, PREFACE JEANNE BOURIN 1995 *The Book of Chocolate.* Paris, New York: Flammarion.
BLYTHMAN, JOANNA 1996 *The Food We Eat.* London: Michael Joseph.
COADY, CHANTAL 1993 *Chocolate: The Food of the Gods.* London: Pavilion Books.
COADY, CHANTAL 1995 *The Chocolate Companion.* London: Quintet Publishing.
COE, SOPHIE D. AND MICHAEL D. 1996 *The True History of Chocolate.* London: Thames and Hudson.
COX, CAT 1993 *Chocolate Unwrapped: The Politics of Pleasure.* London: The Women's Environmental Network.
GAGE, THOMAS 1648 *The English-American His Travail by Land and Sea, or a New Survey of the West Indies.* London.
HEAD, BRANDON 1905 *The Food of the Gods.* London: George Routledge & Sons.

McGEE, HAROLD 1984 *On Food and Cooking: The Science and Lore of the Kitchen.* London, Australia: George Allen & Unwin.
MONTIGNAC, MICHEL 1991 *Dine Out and Lose Weight.* London: Artulen UK.
RICHART DESIGN ET CHOCOLAT *Le Petit Livre Blanc du Chocolat.*
SHERR, JEREMY *The Homoeopathic Proving of Chocolate.* Dynamis School.
Spicing up the Palate: Studies of Flavourings — Ancient and Modern. Proceedings of the Oxford Symposium on Food and Cookery 1992. Totnes, Devon: Prospect Books.
STOBART, TOM 1977 *Herbs, Spices and Flavourings.* Penguin Books.
TRAGER, JAMES 1995 *The Food Chronology.* Ontario: Fitzhenry & Whiteside.
WATERHOUSE, DEBRA 1995 *Why Women Need Chocolate.* London: Vermilion.
WHYMPER, R. 1921 *Cocoa and Chocolate: Their Chemistry and Manufacture.* London: J. & A. Churchill.
WILLIAMS, C. TREVOR 1953 *Chocolate and Confectionery.* London.